JONAH

A DEVOTIONAL REFLECTION

ROSS KINGWELL, PH.D.

WESTBOW
PRESS®
A DIVISION OF THOMAS NELSON
& ZONDERVAN

WestBow Press books may be ordered through booksellers or by contacting:

WestBow Press
A Division of Thomas Nelson & Zondervan
1663 Liberty Drive
Bloomington, IN 47403
www.westbowpress.com
1 (866) 928-1240

ISBN: 978-1-5127-9633-9 (sc)
ISBN: 978-1-5127-9632-2 (hc)
ISBN: 978-1-5127-9634-6 (e)

Library of Congress Control Number: 2017910937

Print information available on the last page.

WestBow Press rev. date: 7/19/2017

CONTENTS

LIST OF FIGURES

INTRODUCTION

The book of Jonah is grand drama unfolding in only forty-eight verses. It is a story of God's broad and enduring care contrasted against the deeply-felt, different views of Jonah, God's prophet. It is a book often remembered more for the unusual elements of its drama rather than for the messages of the drama. Being inquisitive beings often our gaze fixes on the bizarre and unusual rather than seeing beyond them to their Author and purpose.

In a devotional rather than strict scholarly context, the following chapters highlight some of the riches of the book of Jonah, drawing on the comments and views of commentators and scholars who have contributed to an appreciation of the book.

In the following sections first the nature of the book, the life and times of Jonah and the unusual natural events of the book are described briefly. Then observations and devotional notes accompany a listing of the text of the Book of Jonah. A final section offers closing comments.

NATURE OF THE BOOK

The literary classification of the book of Jonah is a difficulty. Biblical scholars are divided and three main views exist. The Who's Who supporting the view that the book is an historical account includes Josephus, almost all the Church Fathers, Jerome, Calvin, Keil-Delitzsch, Barnes, Laetsch and Kendall. Another impressive list supporting a view that the book is a parable includes Luther, Pfeiffer, the compilers of the Jerusalem Bible and Leslie Allen. The final viewpoint shared mainly by some twentieth century scholars, like Smith, Knight and Smart, is that the book is an allegory.

Crean (2002) makes the useful observation that chapter two in the book of Jonah is an example of religious poetry but the rest of the book belongs to the genre of popular narrative and *not* that of learned history. Crean argues, however, that use of the genre of popular narrative does not prove that the events related are invented rather than real.

I am not equipped with the scholarship skills to dissect helpfully the argument and counter-argument surrounding the nature of the book, except to point out some of the difficulties inherent in each viewpoint. Those who favour the view that the book describes historical events face the difficulty of conceding that some main events in the book are highly unlikely and more likely to be miraculous. That a man overboard would be swallowed by a great fish is unlikely: that he would then survive a three day stay (not strictly 72 hours but nonetheless many hours) in a great fish is very highly improbable if not miraculous. The next difficulty is the seemingly supernatural growth rate achieved by the plant that sheltered Jonah. Finally, it is a much mentioned fact that the extensive Assyrian records, as discovered to date, nowhere mention Jonah or Nineveh's repentance. Certainly the silence of the Assyrian records is consistent with the book of Jonah not being history but it is not sufficient evidence to dismiss claims for the book's historicity as James Smith makes the observation that "the history of Assyria during the period of Jonah is virtually a blank."[1] Hence it is not that Assyrian records are especially silent regarding Jonah but rather Assyrian records are as yet uncited for the period of history when Jonah was likely to have lived.

For some who see the book of Jonah not as history mostly do so because of their assessment of its literary style. For example, the author and academic, C.S. Lewis comments about the book that it is "a tale with as few even pretended historical attachments as Job, grotesque in incident and surely not without a distinct, though of course edifying, vein of typically Jewish humour."[2] However, elsewhere Lewis does say "I never regard any narrative as unhistorical simply on the ground that it includes the miraculous."[3]

The book of Jonah's internal evidence to support its historical accuracy is scant. There is no mention of who was reigning in the kingdom when Jonah departed Israel, yet the reference from 2 Kings would indicate that Jeroboam was the king. Even the mention of Tarshish is somewhat indecisive. The word Tarshish has a Semitic root 'to smelt' suggesting a town where smelting occurred. There is a likelihood that such smelting was possible at several locations in the Mediterranean, although it is currently believed that Tarshish was in Spain and was the western furthest point in the then known world of the Israelites.

A difficulty facing the supporters of the parable and allegory viewpoints concerns the interpretation of Matthew 12:41 and Luke 11:32. Using Matthew 12:41 as the example, Jesus Christ is reputed to say — "The men of Nineveh will stand up at the judgement with this generation and condemn it; for they repented at the preaching of Jonah, and now one greater than Jonah is here."

The parable and allegory viewpoints would deny the historicity of Nineveh's repentance as described in the book of Jonah. Yet if Matthew 12:41 is accepted as an accurate report of Christ's words, then one possible

---

[1] *Obadiah, Joel, Jonah, Micah: A Christian Interpretation*, (Florida Christian College, 2011), 143.

[2] *Christian Reflections* (Ed: W. Hooper) (Collins, Fount Paperbacks, 1967), 194.

[3] *Reflections on the Psalms* (Fontana Books, 1958), 94.

interpretation of His words is that He was stating an historical fact that the Ninevites did repent at the preaching of Jonah.

However, the supporters of the parable and allegory viewpoints would interpret Matthew 12:41 differently. Various interpretations are possible. The reported words of Christ may not be his exact words but are some interpolation. Christ may have used His audience's view that the book of Jonah was history as a means to reflect to them God's judgement of them. But this raises a thorny issue; if Christ knew the events in the book of Jonah were only a parable and not history, would He then imply support for the people's view of the book of Jonah as history by saying what He did? In spite of this question Leslie Allen points out: "allowance must be made for a figurative element in the teaching of Christ, an element Western literalists have notoriously found difficulty in grasping. If a modern preacher would not be at fault if he challenged his congregation with a reference to Lady Macbeth or Oliver Twist, could not Jesus have eluded in much the same manner to a well-known story to reinforce his own distinctive message?"[4]

Smith (2011) argues oppositely that the biblical tradition is to view the book as history. The book of Tobit, written during the intertestamental period, considered the book of Jonah as history as did the Jewish historian Josephus. Smith also lists the main reasons why the book is viewed as history or not. The most ancient references to the book of Jonah in Jewish literatures suggest that it was always understood as historical. Beck (2000) outlines the various interpretive traditions of the biblical narrative of Jonah among Jews and Christians from the mid-second century BC through to the end of the fifth century AD. Interestingly, Beck points out archaeological investigations in Rome that reveal Jonah was a dominant religious symbol of hope for Christians. Among the catacombs' funerary art dated prior to the emperor Constantine, a third display the story of Jonah and the great fish. Hence, the story and meaning of Jonah was very popular among Rome's Christians.

As a further aside, it is worth noting that the book of Jonah continues to this day to be part of the most solemn of days in the Jewish calendar. The book of Jonah is read on Yom Kippur (the Day of Atonement), the

---

[4] *The Books of Joel, Obadiah, Jonah and Micah*, (Wiiliam B. Eerdmans Publishing Co, 1976), 180.

holiest day of the year in Judaism. The book is read in its entirety on the afternoon of Yom Kippur. The day is observed with fasting, intensive prayer and attendance at synagogue services. Yom Kippur is the day for remembering and seeking reconciliation with God and people. Two main reasons are given for reading the book of Jonah at the Yom Kippur afternoon services. Firstly, the book illustrates that no one is beyond the reach of God and secondly, that no matter the nature of our past behaviour, God's benevolence and mercy awaits those who genuinely repent.

My own views regarding the book of Jonah have changed over the years. As a younger man I only saw the book as history. Now I am less certain. I find many comments made by supporters of the history, parable and allegory viewpoints to be relevant and helpful to a study of the book, even if I remain unconvinced of some other of their arguments. When examining the book I've tried to empathise with the person of Jonah experiencing the events described, be they historical or fiction. As in any great work of non-fiction or fiction, it is possible to be moved by the events and people and learn from them.

Of concern to me are some blunt comments of some proponents of the historical view who choose to judge and condemn those who fail to share their view. By illustration is the comment of Hailey (1972) who suggested that a person's ability or inability to accept a miracle depended on whether or not they spelled their God with a capital 'G'. His comment suggests that those who view the book of Jonah as history believe in a powerful God able to act miraculously, whereas the non-believers in the historicity don't actually consider these miracles occurred, implying their God lacks omnipotence which is not necessarily true. To support the book's historicity by attacking others with different views is concerning. Are we not told that the work of God's Spirit is love and gentleness? (Galatians 5:22,23). Although the defence of truth is always meritorious, often humility, care and thorough diligence are the best company on the path to truth; and yet even then, some things we may never know and we should be honest enough to say so.

My advice, for what it's worth, is that when you come to make your own assessment of the literary classification of the book, don't let either the uncertainty of its classification or the unusual nature of its events become impediments to understanding the book's broad and rich lessons.

THE LIFE AND TIMES OF JONAH

In the Old Testament, apart from the book of Jonah, there is only one other reference to Jonah in 2 Kings 14:25. This single verse links Jonah to the reign of Jeroboam II a king of Israel in the first half of the eighth century BC. The verse is a vital key to understanding and interpreting much of the later reported behaviour of Jonah —

> "He (*Jeroboam II*) was the one who restored the boundaries of Israel from Lebo Hamath to the Sea of Arabah, in accordance with the word of the LORD, the God of Israel, spoken through his servant Jonah son of Amittai, the prophet from Gath Hepher." (2 Kings 14:25)

Read in the wider context of surrounding verses in 2 Kings chapter 14, the picture emerges that the people of Israel were experiencing a bitter suffering (verse 26). The cause of their pain is not specified. Possible explanations offered by some commentators are the internal exploitation of Israelites by Jeroboam and his courtiers who were profligate and treacherously selfish; and the external oppression of Israel by marauding bands of Syrians who pillaged villages in northern Israel. Whatever the cause of their distress, we do know, based on what is written in 2 Kings 14, that God responded by restoring the boundaries of Israel through the leadership of Jeroboam II.

It is worth noting that Jeroboam II was God's agent in relieving Israel's suffering in spite of Jeroboam being one of the many kings in the Old Testament summarily described as having done "evil in the eyes of the Lord." He continued the errors of one of his predecessors, Jeroboam

I, and as such, shared in God's judgement of Jeroboam's house that was afflicted with the sword (Amos 7:9). Zechariah, Jeroboam II's son reigned for only six months before he was murdered. The royal line of Jeroboam's house was severed, never regaining power (2 Kings 15:8–12).

Jonah's role in providing relief to Israel was to serve as God's prophet and announce this good news: Israel's lands were to be restored! In Israel's largely agrarian culture where ownership or access to land mattered much, such an enlargement implied relief from other neighbours keen to occupy or plunder Israel's lands. It also widened the geographical base of Israel's natural resources and potentially improved its food security. The extent of the territorial enlargement was impressive with borders restored from the "entrance of Hamath" (the northern end of the Beqaa Valley in Syria) to the "Sea of the Arabah" (i.e. the Dead Sea).

From verse 25 in 2 Kings 14 we learn some personal details about Jonah. Firstly, his name *Jonah* means dove. Insofar as a person's name in the Old Testament often conveys meaning about the person, then there are a few interpretations to Jonah being a dove. It may symbolize Jonah as a message-carrier, one in flight for God, bringing God's peace, like the dove in the story of Noah. Also, it may typify Jonah as Israel, for Israel was later symbolically called dove (Hosea 11:11).

Next, we learn that his father's name was *Amittai* (means truth or faithfulness) and that he was a prophet from Gath Hepher. As a prophet he followed in the tradition of Elijah and Elisha. Indeed, ancient texts and traditions link Jonah to both these prophets. Delitzsch refers to an ancient Haggada which says Jonah was one of the sons of the prophets belonging to Elisha's school of prophets. Keil refers to Jerome and others who describe Jewish traditions that Jonah was the son of the widow at Zarephath whom Elijah restored to life. Scripture itself is silent on the links, if any, between Jonah and Elijah or Elisha.

To be a prophet was to be God's mouthpiece. As God's servants prophets were required to be obedient and to convey God's words wherever and to whosoever He directed. God commanded Ezekiel, for example, to speak the words God gave to him, irrespective of whether people listened or not (Ezekiel 2:7). It is known that some prophets took solemn vows binding them to God's service. Being God's servant as prophet was rarely an easy task. Often they were unpopular, abused and, at times, lived in danger. By contrast, however, Jonah's role in announcing Israel's restoration possibly lifted him into the limelight of national fame and gratitude. One commentator even suggests that in this regard Jonah was a statesman. Statesman or not, at least Jonah's pronouncements would have lifted his popularity.

Jonah came from Gath Hepher. The town's name means well by the wine press, indicative of the region's agricultural nature. The town was located in the tribal land of Zebulun; a land of rolling plain, agriculturally productive and beautiful. According to the New Bible Dictionary the people of Zebulun had a reputation for patriotism. For example, at one time when the tribes of Israel were called to the defence of Israel (Judges 5:18) only Zebulun and Naphtali came. In 1 Chronicles 12 only the tribe of Zebulun is described as being undivided in its loyalty to king David. The land of Zebulun was a small area to the west of the Sea of Galilee (Chinnereth) and was one of a handful of tribal lands that shared borders solely with other tribes of Israel. It was a pocket of Jews surrounded by Jews — perhaps an enabling geographical recipe for patriotism. To the north and east lay the tribal land of Naphtali, to the west Asher and to the east and south were Issachar and to the south was Manasseh (see map 1).

Nazareth and Gath Hepher lie in the Israelite tribal territory of Zebulun about a hundred kilometres north of Jerusalem, nearly half-way between the Mediterranean Sea and the Sea of Galilee (Chinnereth). Gath Hepher was a small town about four kilometres northeast of Nazareth, so it lay within walking distance of Nazareth (see map 2).

Jerome mentions a tomb of Jonah at Gath Hepher, so I find it quite credible to envisage that, if the tomb did exist, Jesus as a young man may have visited it and possibly reflected on the person and message of Jonah. Even if the tomb did not exist it is highly likely that Jesus would have visited Gath Hepher, solely due to its proximity to Nazareth and may well have pondered upon the story of Jonah.

It is worth highlighting that Jonah was the only minor prophet Christ mentions directly (Matthew 12:39–41; 16:4; Luke 11:29–32). The name Jonah was also the name of Simon Peter's father (Matthew 16:17) and Jesus specifically calls Peter, "Simon son of Jonah" when he first declares Jesus to be the Christ, the Son of the living God (Matthew 16:16). Peter's father was a linguistic reminder to Christ and all His disciples of Jonah the prophet.

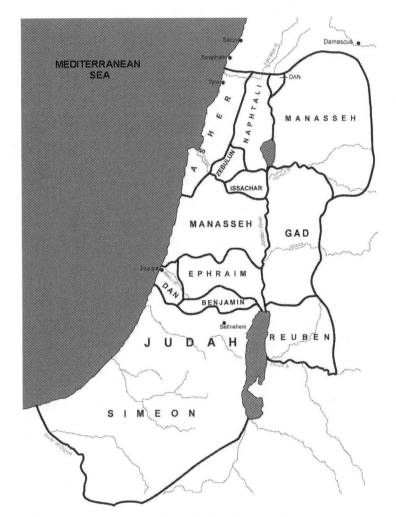

Map 1: The tribal lands of Israel

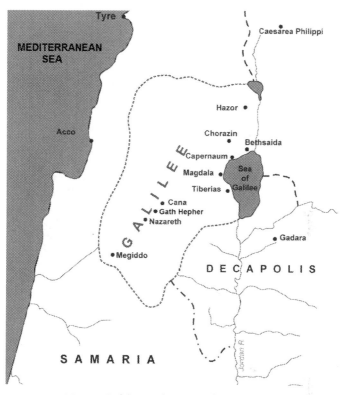

Map 2: Galilee in the time of Jesus Christ

Much of Christ's ministry was in the various towns of Zebulun and the adjacent tribal land of Naphtali. Zebulun and Naphtali are among the few tribal lands specifically mentioned in the gospels. For example, Matthew 4:12–17 describes how Christ went from Nazareth in Zebulun to live in Capernaum in Naphtali, specifically to fulfil the prophecy in Isaiah 8:23 to Isaiah 9:3 regarding the lands of Zebulun and Naphtali.

Historically, biblical scholars consider that the Jonah in 2 Kings 14:25 is the same Jonah in the book bearing his name; if different it is remarkable that both are prophets and both have the same father's name (see Jonah 1:1). These biblical scholars, including those supporting a parable or allegory viewpoint, confer on the Jonah in the book of his name a patriotic fervour that could well typify someone from Zebulun and be consistent with the little we know of the Jonah in 2 Kings 14:25. Like these scholars I will draw upon the information in 2 Kings 14:25 in discussing the behaviour of Jonah in the book of Jonah.

NATURAL DIFFICULTIES

Before discussing the biblical text of Jonah, I should raise the difficulties surrounding the big fish and the fast-growing plant, lest they become impediments to understanding the main lessons of Jonah. I would stress that they are only difficulties for those who see the events as history; but even then some who accept the book as history are also confident and comfortable that God directed so many miracles.

> And the Lord appointed a great fish to swallow up Jonah;
> and Jonah was in the belly of the fish three days and three
> nights. (Jonah 1:17, ESV)

In reflection; it is a sad commentary upon myself, and perhaps some other readers of this verse, that at times we have lingered too long to ponder over the unusual event of a great fish swallowing a man, rather than on the Lord who arranged it all; "And the *Lord appointed* a great fish to swallow up Jonah" (verse 17a).

Hebrew versions of this verse refer to a great fish; Greek versions use a word meaning a huge sea monster; and English versions speak of a fish or great fish. However, in the Greek versions of Matthew 12:40 where Christ speaks of being three days and three nights in the heart of the earth as Jonah was three days and three nights in the great fish — the Greek word for great fish usually means whale or sea-monster. Hence, in translating Matthew 12:40 the King James' version and the Revised Standard version use the word "whale", while the Revised English Bible and Bishop Weymouth use the words "sea-monster's belly". In short, the association of Jonah with a whale arises out of some New Testament translations.

In Jonah 1:17 where we first read of the great fish we also read that God appointed or prepared the fish. The Hebrew word that we translate as "appointed" or "prepared" is different from the word "created". The implication is that the great fish was already in existence and was not some special creature that God instantaneously created for the occasion.

To support the view that the swallowing of Jonah by a great fish is historical, various scholars and commentators (e.g. Henry 2012) have relayed other accounts of people being swallowed by great fish — not all accounts being factual as Leslie Allen discusses in his commentary on Jonah. Two accounts are commonly related. For example, Keil-Delitzsch relate a story, more elaborately described by Muller, in which in 1758 a soldier travelling on a frigate in the Mediterranean fell overboard amid very stormy weather. The man was immediately taken into the mouth of a carcharias. This apparently is a shark that can grow to eight metres in length and can have about four hundred lance-shaped teeth arranged in six rows and which can be elevated or depressed. Like many other sharks it has a voracious appetite eating plaice, seals and tunny fish and in this instance a person! The captain ordered a deck gun to fire immediately at the shark. A cannon ball struck the shark causing the soldier to be disgorged still alive and very little hurt.

Another incident concerns a crew member of a whaling ship stationed near the Falkland Islands in the South Atlantic. The crewman was swallowed by a sperm whale. After three days he was recovered from its stomach, unconscious, but alive. Interestingly, the gastric juices had bleached his skin. Apparently, there is even an instance of a whole horse being found in the belly of one of them.

Although the first of these two accounts may be undisputed, the second incident relayed by Keil-Delitzsch has been found to be a hoax (See Allen 1976 and Davis 1991). Nonetheless the imagined incident is often falsely re-stated as if true.

Even if actual verified examples are found, they would simply reinforce how very unlikely and bizarre such a swallowing and survival would be. When mentioning such stories some commentators acknowledge that the carcharias and the sperm whale are found in the Mediterranean, and in previous centuries were far more common-place than now. The fact that Jonah was vomited out on shore (Jonah 2:10) is also seen by many as consistent with the behaviour of some whales which en masse occasionally beach themselves.

Disbelief is not a recent phenomenon regarding this unlikely sequence that firstly, a sea creature could swallow Jonah and secondly, that he would then survive the lengthy ordeal only to be regurgitated safely on a shore. In 409 AD, Augustine of Hippo wrote to Deogratias concerning the challenge of some to the miracle of Jonah. He wrote of the criticism and quoted it:

> …. what are we to believe concerning Jonah, who is said to have been three days in a whale's belly? The thing is utterly improbable and incredible, that a man swallowed with his clothes on should have existed in the inside of a fish. If, however, the story is figurative, be pleased to explain it. Again, what is meant by the story that a gourd sprang up above the head of Jonah after he was vomited by the fish? What was the cause of this gourd's growth?" Questions such as these I have seen discussed by Pagans amidst loud laughter, and with great scorn. (Letter CII, Section 30)

As mentioned by Augustine, another natural difficulty in the book of Jonah is the fast-growing plant. The relevant verses are Jonah 4:6–10, KJV —

> And the Lord God prepared a gourd, and made it to come up over Jonah, that it might be a shadow over his head, to deliver him from his evil. So Jonah was exceeding glad because of the gourd. But God prepared a worm when the morning rose the next day, and it smote the gourd, that it withered. And it came to pass, when the sun arose, that God prepared a vehement east wind; and the sun beat upon the head of Jonah, that he fainted, and requested for himself that he might die, and said: 'It is

better for me to die than live.' And God said to Jonah:
'Art thou greatly angry for the gourd?' And he said: 'I
am greatly angry, even unto death.' And the Lord said:
'Thou hast had pity on the gourd, for which thou hast
not laboured, neither madest it grow, which came up in
a night, and perished in a night:'

The phrase in verse 10 translated as "which came up in a night, and perished in a night" literally means "which was the son of a night and perished a son of the night." It is a Hebrew figurative phrase for perished rapidly. To see the plant's growth and death as history may mean that in a single day the plant grew to a sufficient height to shade Jonah as he sat in his booth; in which case the growth of the plant is not just unusual or unlikely, as with Jonah's swallowing, but is almost certainly miraculous. However, the text describing the plant's life may also be interpreted to give the plant a longer and natural growth, albeit appointed by God, while still aptly describing the plant as having perished rapidly.

Explaining further; Jonah's message to the Ninevites was "In forty days Nineveh shall be destroyed." Having delivered this message he waited on the east side of the city to see what became of it. The fact that he made a booth for himself suggests that he may have envisaged a long wait, perhaps many days. And while he waited, He waited. God first provided a plant to shade him and in response Jonah "was exceeding glad because of the gourd." But on the next day God provided a worm that fed on the gourd and killed it, thereby removing Jonah's shade.

One question over the timing of events is whether or not the plant's growth sufficient to provide shade and Jonah's gladness for the shade occurred on the same day, or whether or not the plant grew naturally and then Jonah became glad for its shade? An associated question is; did God appoint the worm to kill the plant the day after Jonah was exceedingly glad or the day after the plant started growing? As I see it, there are two main answers or options available. Firstly, the plant's growth and death occurred in two days in which case almost certainly a miraculous growth event occurred. Secondly, the plant grew naturally but the day after Jonah was exceedingly glad for its shade the plant died; yet the plant still being aptly described as having perished rapidly.

Of interest to scholars who see the book of Jonah as history is the botanical nature of the plant. The book of Jonah does not give the plant a clear botanical name yet some scholars speculate the plant is the vine or bottle gourd *Curcurbita lagenaria*. They observe that shepherds would often carry the seeds of the bottle gourd and plant some at the base of their humpies to provide shade. A few other scholars say the plant could have been the castor-oil plant.

I turn now to the text of the book of Jonah, moving through it section by section. Unless otherwise stated, the New International Version is the translation source.

JONAH CHAPTER ONE

The word of the LORD came to Jonah son of Amittai:

"Go to the great city of Nineveh and preach against it, because its wickedness has come up before me."

But Jonah ran away from the LORD and headed for Tarshish. He went down to Joppa, where he found a ship bound for that port. After paying the fare, he went aboard and sailed for Tarshish to flee from the LORD. (Jonah 1:1–3)

COMMENTS

The book begins with the "word of the LORD" coming to Jonah. Assuming that the Jonah son of Amittai here is the same Jonah son of Amittai in 2 Kings 14:25, then this Jonah has heard the word of the Lord before. He is no child Samuel, hearing God speaking for the first time (1 Samuel 3:4–5). As a prophet, Jonah has some familiarity with God's words. He has at least once before heard God's words and served God obediently by speaking them to Israel. Furthermore, he would know from Israel's history, if not from personal experience that, comforting though God's words can be, they can also be weighty and arresting, and therefore not always welcome. Yet because they are God's words and because he is a prophet, Jonah is obliged to be obedient and to speak them as God directs.

It is perhaps worth pausing for reflection at this early point in the book of Jonah, as much of what people know and say of Jonah is due to his and God's actions after verse one. Staying with verse 1, however, it is worth highlighting what is commendable about Jonah at this point of time in his interaction with God.

Jonah is *available* to God. He does *hear* God. He *knows* that God is speaking. And he does *understand* what God is requesting. All those features of Jonah's initial interaction with God are commendable. It is ever so easy to rush through verse 1, chasing the narrative and thus forgetting to pause and dwell on Jonah and the soundness and richness of this initial interaction with God. He was available to God, able to hear Him, able to know that He spoke. And, significantly, he was able to understand what God said. Jonah, at this point, illustrates faith in that "faith cometh by hearing, and hearing by the word of God." (Romans 10:17).

Yet remember, there are examples in Scripture where God speaks and people do not know that He is speaking. For example, Samuel hears the voice of God but thinks it is Eli who speaks (1 Samuel 3:4–5). God speaks to the Egyptian king via a dream, but the king needs Joseph to interpret to him what God is saying (Genesis 41). The resurrected Christ talks to two of his followers on the road to Emmaus, but they do not know until He breaks bread with them that the Son of God has been speaking to them (Luke 24:13–35). Yet here, Jonah hears, knows and understands that God speaks. And as we learn later in verse 2 of chapter 4, Jonah also has other confidences in God.

It is rare for most people to know with clarity and confidence the exact will of God in any particular situation. In that respect, Jonah is very different from most people in that he hears, knows and understands that God is speaking. That Jonah is enabled to hear, know and understand says much about the calibre of his relationship with God. How Jonah arrives at that confidence and facility in his relationship with God is not revealed by the text. How a person arrives at such a confidence is an entirely separate study of many other parts of scripture. Yet here in verse 1 of chapter 1 of the book of Jonah it is revealed that it is possible for a person to have such a confidence in recognising the instruction of God.

Another point to note about the opening verses of the book of Jonah is that we, as readers, are exposed to Jonah's reaction to having heard God. Unfortunately, I would assert, this is not a common feature of the societies in which most of us might live. Our experience is more likely to be filled with people reacting to other people, their immediate environment, and their circumstances rather than primarily reacting to God. Hence, we are privileged to read and learn from a reaction to hearing God.

The story of Jonah mostly is known by the key aspects of his story. Many people link Jonah to his disobedience or his being swallowed by a sea creature. He is remembered as a noun in the dictionary: a Jonah. That is, a person regarded as bringing bad luck. Few people remember him at his beginning when there was no disobedience, when he was blessed in being enabled to hear God. We remember what happened *to* him, not what happened *with* him or *in* him or *in spite of* him.

Another reflection on the opening verses of the book of Jonah is to note that we, as readers, are given clarity over what God says. By contrast, in the book of Esther what God says is absent. The name of God is never mentioned in that book. Yet here in the book of Jonah we have the useful opportunity to hear (as Jonah heard) what God says. In addition, we subsequently have the opportunity to see what God does and learn why He does what He does. Furthermore, we have the opportunity to see reaction to what God says and does.

In the opening verses of Jonah, God instructs Jonah to go to Nineveh. However, Jonah does not — for reasons described shortly.

God's words are firstly to Jonah as His prophet and secondly to the city of Nineveh. For its time, Nineveh was a huge city with a long history. Back in Genesis we read of its founder Asshur (Genesis 10:11) and by Jonah's time the city had become a centre of the Assyrian empire. In Jonah 3:3 and Jonah 4:11 are other indicators of the city's size, the latter verse implying that the city had more than 120,000 young children (that is, those unable to distinguish between their right and left hands).

The current ruins of Nineveh stand not far from the modern city of Mosul (Al-Mawsil) in northern Iraq (see map 3) and are located midway from the borders of Syria and Iran. Nineveh was already an ancient and important royal city when Sennacherib (704–681 BC) designated it the imperial capital. Sennacherib enlarged the city from an area of approximately 150 hectares to an unprecedented 750 hectares by the time of its destruction in 612 BC (Stronach 1994).

Although located near the Tigris River, due to the size of its population, Nineveh was dependent on a sophisticated canal system built by Sennacherib. Over fifteen years he oversaw construction of canals that provided water to Nineveh and its surrounding areas for irrigated agriculture. Initially a thirteen kilometre canal, the Kisiri canal, was built behind Nineveh then the massive Northern and Khinis canal systems were constructed, the latter stretching almost one hundred kilometres, involving over fifty kilometres of excavated canals, and including at least one aqueduct requiring an estimated two million cut blocks (Wilkinson et al. 2005). Near Nineveh the main canal delivering water was up to twenty-two metres wide and two metres deep. At Nineveh, Sennacherib simulated the forests of the Amanus Mountains of Anatolia in a park just beyond the city wall, and he arrested the flow of the Khosr River to create a Babylonian marsh, complete with reeds and pigs (Jacobsen and Lloyd 1935). Like his predecessors, he filled Nineveh and the villages of its hinterland with the forcibly deported populations of conquered lands.

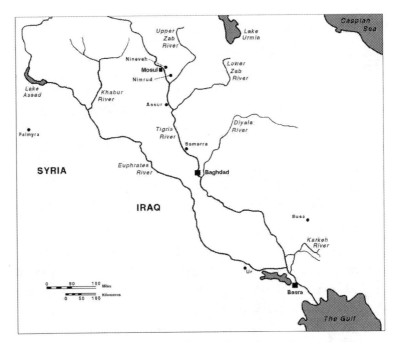

Map 3: The ruins of the city of Nineveh are located near the Tigris river. The adjacent city of Mosul is also known al-Mawsil.

However, it was not the size, engineering or architectural splendour of Nineveh that brought response from God. It was the wickedness of its inhabitants. In the Old Testament, the word we translate as wicked is used in two senses. Firstly, it has a judicial meaning insofar as a person is judged wicked or righteous. Secondly, it has a behavioural meaning in that a person can do evil or be perverse or make mischief. Although this verse in Jonah seems to emphasize the behavioural wickedness of Nineveh, the legal meaning nonetheless would also apply.

Smith (2011) makes the helpful observation that the wickedness of Nineveh included idolatry and pride (Isaiah 10:5–19, 36:8–20), cruel oppression (2 Kings 15:29, 17:6; Isaiah 36:16–17), and especially inhumane warfare. What we know of Assyrian or Ninevite behaviour from sources outside scripture certainly identifies their behaviour as idolatrous, but more especially cruel and rapacious.

From the time of Ashurnasirpal II (883–859 BC) Assyrians relied on cruelty to acquire and hold down territory. Ashurnasirpal II's usual procedure after the capture of a hostile city was to burn it and then to mutilate all the grown male prisoners by cutting off their hands and ears and putting out their eyes. Then the men were piled up in a great heap to perish in agony from their wounds, the harsh sun, and suffocation. The children, both boys and girls, were all burnt alive at the stake. The city's chief, if alive, was carried off to the Assyrian capital to be flayed for the king's pleasure.

There is a gruesome passage in John Hercus's book *More Pages from God's Case-Book* in which he describes other sorts of Assyrian brutality —

> Taking captive hostages from one conquered city, they would tie them in naked strings with ropes round their necks, or with iron bits forced into their mouths, and lead them to the gates of the next town to be attacked. And there, before the terrified gaze of the citizens peering over the walls, these miserable wretches would be hoisted up as human pennants on great Assyrian stakes thrust through the mid-riff. And as the victims writhed in their death throes, the Assyrian spokesman would bellow his demand for surrender, warning the fear stricken onlookers of an equal or worse fate if they dared resist. (1965, 26)[5]

---

[5] *More Pages from God's Case-book*, (IVF: London, 1965), 26.

Graphic 1: Relief of Tiglath-pileser

In some Assyrian houses curtains were made of human flesh and lamp holders from human bones; such was their disregard for humanity. Assyrians were renowned for terror and violence toward enemies. Assyrian monuments testify their brutality as shown by the above illustration depicting Tiglath-pileser III besieging a city with bodies of dead enemies impaled and lifted up in fearful display. In the book of

Nahum which tells of Nineveh's eventual destruction by God we read of Nineveh being *a* "bloody city....full of lies and robbery" (Nahum 3:1) and later, "All who hear the news of you clap their hands at your downfall. For who has not felt your unrelenting cruelty?" (Nahum 3:19).

The Interpreters' Dictionary of the Bible comments that Nineveh was regarded by Jews of the stricter sort as a synonym for the worst infamies, vicious practices, blasphemy and irreligion of the Gentile world. So it was to Nineveh, the main Assyrian capital, that Jonah was commanded to go with God's words. But Jonah, rather than heading north-east to Nineveh, went to Joppa (south-west from Zebulun) then westwards towards Tarshish. The town of Tarshish, most scholars agree, was probably Tartessus in the south-west of Spain that maintained a mineral trade with Tyre and, according to one commentator, could have been an ancient Semitic colony.

Jonah's departure to Tarshish is both a deliberate and a multi-staged action. It required him to leave Israel and, in particular, Zebulun; a difficult choice if he was strongly patriotic. It required journeying first to Joppa, then searching for and finding a departing vessel. It involved the financial cost of travel to Joppa, a fare to Tarshish and perhaps money for later expenses in Tarshish or in ports along the way. It required Jonah, a Jew accustomed to living among Jews, to reside with foreigners in an entirely new land and to be cut off from family and friends. It probably involved danger, for Tarshish in Jonah's era was the other end of the world, and the seas could well be rough and hazardous on part of such a long journey. Lastly, it required him going from honour, acknowledgment and possibly fame in Gath Hepher and Zebulun as God's prophet to relative anonymity in Tarshish.

Within the few words, "He went down to Joppa, where he found a ship bound for Tarshish. After paying the fare, he went aboard and sailed for Tarshish", is hidden the personal cost and emotion that Jonah must have experienced in deciding to flee. People rarely give up their country, their family ties, their home, and their occupation that often is a source of their personal status, on a whim. Jonah's departure was not some small slip or one single act of transgression. It was a deliberate set and sequence of actions. His reasons for fleeing would not be trite or arise from a weak motivation. In Jonah 4:2 we are given some insights into those reasons.

I pray Thee, O Lord, was not this what I said when I was
yet in my country? Therefore I fled before unto Tarshish;
for I knew that Thou art a gracious God and merciful,
slow to anger and of great kindness, and repentest of the
evil. (Jonah 4:2, KJV)

When you read Jonah 1:1–3 in isolation, it seems as if no conversation
occurred between Jonah and God. Put simply, God spoke and Jonah fled.
However, Jonah 4:2 makes clear that there was conversation, or at least
complaint from Jonah.

Before we rush to condemn the disobedience of Jonah by not going to
Nineveh, we should note that he was spiritually mature enough to know,
firstly, that God would listen to his complaint and secondly, that what he
knew and said about God was true. (Sometimes, by comparison, I am far
less mature than Jonah insofar as I say things about God not true of Him
or I'm not yet aware of things about Him.)

When scholars and commentators have pondered over Jonah 4:2,
what do they conclude as to the reason why Jonah fled to Tarshish?
Jacques Ellul considers Jonah fled in fear of his life. Telling the capital of
a nation renowned for cruelty that it was doomed was a recipe for self-
endangerment. A violent and cruel people may well be violent and cruel
to Jonah; especially given that he was a foreigner daring to scare a fearless
people. Calvin thinks that Jonah fled because he was afraid he would seem
like a false prophet and that this would also badly reflect on God, as if
God was not consistent with His word. Calvin's idea about Jonah fearing
to be seen as a false prophet has some credence, if one assumes that Jonah
greatly valued being known in Israel as a true prophet. If people in Israel
learned that the words that Jonah spoke in Nineveh were not fulfilled,
then the admiration he received from Israelites would lessen. Some would
brand him a false prophet and his high standing would be tarnished.
Hugh Martin supports Calvin by saying that Jonah was afraid lest, by
the Ninevites repenting and God remitting the threatened punishment,
that God might be regarded as a changeable God. Luther suggests that
Jonah fled in fear because of the novelty of the prophetic message. There
is also some merit in Luther's idea of novelty. Prophecies of judgement
of Gentile nations were proclaimed usually in Israel and said particularly

for the ears of Israel. God's words to Nineveh were indeed novel because not only were they to be said in Nineveh, but it seemed the words were for Nineveh for its own sake.

However the majority of commentators — people like Jerome, Keil-Delitzsch, Henry, Laetsch, Gaebelein and Kendall — all testify that Jonah fled in fear of the Ninevites being spared God's threatened blow. When Jonah thought of Nineveh he saw a dreadful cruel foe needing a severe crushing. He was already filled with the spirit of Nahum, ready to clap his hands at the long-overdue news of Nineveh's demise. In his thinking, bad behaviour deserved a bad end. For God to spare Nineveh and overlook its brutal history was inappropriate softness. How could God spare Israel's enemy or overlook the suffering which Nineveh unleashed? Was the God of Israel truly for Israel? Jonah's position was clear. He was for Israel. He was for Zebulun, not Nineveh. Had he participated in Israel's territorial gain only to see that jeopardized by God's limpness with Nineveh, the enemy of Israel?

Jonah was not against Nineveh because he was racist, in the sense of abhorring anyone not Jewish. After all, he was prepared to journey with Gentiles to Tarshish and live at Tarshish among Gentiles. Also, he would know from the experience of Elijah being sent to a Gentile, the widow at Zaraphath, that prophets can be sent to a Gentile. However, it was one thing to share in the comforting of a poor Gentile widow and her son: it was quite another thing to go to Nineveh, a city of cruel Gentiles, and share in their comforting.

Given the many records of Assyrian brutality, I find it easy to imagine that Jonah, as a character of history or fiction, would have spoken with Israelites who knew much about such events. He may either have known of people or known people disfigured by Assyrians. Some commentators go as far to say that Jonah, as a seer (prophet), may have foreseen the destruction of Israel by Assyria. What is known with far more certainty than these speculations is that the sparing by God of such a people was to Jonah a source of profound annoyance that quickly brimmed to very great anger with God.

The best summary of the reasons for Jonah fleeing that I have heard comes from a scripture teacher from my youth. This teacher was greatly wise and said that Jonah's fleeing was due to the problem of the "I". Remember the words of Jonah:

I pray Thee, O Lord, was not this *my* saying, when *I* was
yet in *my* country? (Jonah 4:2, KJV).

In Jonah's parliament the voting strength lay with the "I"s. Jonah
was driven by what *he* wanted, when living in *his* country, by what *he*
considered just, by what *he* saw as being in Israel's interest.

As a reflection, often in our current society, individualism is promoted
or is allowed and supported. The focus for many is often on **me**, **my**
rights, **my** goals, **my** things, **my** wants and **my** needs. That is not to
imply that care for oneself is inappropriate or wrong. But if the sole
and persistent motivation is self-gratification at cost to those and the
environment around us and at cost to what is most precious, then the
"**I**" is a problem. If greed, selfishness or abuse abounds or masquerades
under the guise of supposed legitimacy of satisfying **my** needs then we
experience the problem of the "**I**".

One of T. J. Carlisle's[6] many insightful poems about Jonah says:

> *And Jonah stalked to his shaded seat*
> *and waited for God*
> *to come around*
> *to his way of thinking.*
>
> *and God is still waiting*
> *for a host of Jonahs*
> *in their comfortable houses*
> *to come around*
> *to His way of thinking*

As a reflection I note that God may not send us to a Nineveh and we
may never be asked by God to speak to an entire city. But I can assure
you that at various stages and, in varied ways, God will lead us and enable
us to jettison some attitudes, ambitions, relationships and activities that
impede our walk with Him. The story of Jonah, in part, is a story of how

---

[6] Reprinted with permission from the publisher, Wm. B. Eermans Publishing Company;
all rights reserved.

deep-seated and pervasive some of those attitudes and ambitions can be, and how clear and persistent God is in guarding His walk with people; be they Nineveh, Jonah, you or me.

In Psalm 23 is the wonderful verse "Thou preparest a table before me in the presence of mine enemies." (Psalm 23:5, KJV). Enemies are not just some other people who wish ill on us. Our enemies include all those things that mar our walk with God; and the list is liable to be long, including some attitudes, self-serving ambitions and things we do not acknowledge; even in spite of some other perceptive people noting those things in us. In the face of such enemies, God feeds us, being the Bread of Life (John 6:35); such is His care.

By now you may have wondered, even if Jonah was greatly annoyed that the Ninevites might be spared punishment, why did he have to flee? The answer lies in verse 3 of chapter 1. In the King James, Revised Standard Version and some other translations the phrase "from the presence of the LORD" is used twice. Jonah is fleeing "from the presence of the LORD". What does it mean to flee from the presence of the LORD? The Amplified Version of verse 3 makes clear the meaning:

> But Jonah rose up to flee unto Tarshish from the presence of the LORD [as His prophet] and went down to Joppa; and he found a ship going to Tarshish: so he paid his fare, and went down into it, to go with them unto Tarshish away from being in the presence of the LORD [as His servant and minister] (Jonah 1:3)

In Old Testament times, to stand in the presence of someone was to be under their influence and in certain cases it also meant to act as their official minister (see Jeremiah 15:19; 1 Kings 17:1). Hence to flee from their presence was to discontinue service to that person. Jonah was signalling to God, in an exaggerated way, that he was no longer able or prepared to be God's prophet. Jonah could not be party to Nineveh possibly being spared. So against going to Nineveh was he, that he made plain to God that he would rather be at the end of the world (Tarshish) than in Nineveh, seeing its destruction averted. And to unambiguously show God how serious and affected he was, he set off for Joppa, found a ship going to Tarshish and paid his fare; and in doing so he resigned as God's prophet in Israel. The anger and determination in Jonah must have been intense and deep-seated to drive him to such an outpost as Tarshish, away from the Israel of his youth.

As a last comment about "the presence of the LORD", I should mention the few scholars who consider the phrase refers to God's geographical sovereignty. They consider that Jonah thought God's power was geographically limited, so by leaving Israel Jonah was out of God's reach. However, Jonah's own comments later in the text and other verses in earlier Old Testament books suggest that most Jews were aware of God's extensive sovereignty. For example, later in the book, the prayer of Jonah refers to God's control and jurisdiction over the seas, when Jonah mentions "all your waves and breakers" (Jonah 2:4b). If that be so, then why did Jonah need to leave Zebulun? Could he not just refuse to speak God's words in Nineveh by remaining in Zebulun? Yes, but such is the theatre of the book of Jonah and its seemingly frequent use of exaggeration that fleeing to Tarshish amply and pictorially reveals Jonah's intention to not serve God in Israel nor abide by His intention.

> Then the LORD sent a great wind on the sea, and such a violent storm arose that the ship threatened to break up.
>
> All the sailors were afraid and each cried out to his own god. And they threw the cargo into the sea to lighten the ship. But Jonah had gone below deck, where he lay down and fell into a deep sleep. The captain went to him and said, "How can you sleep? Get up and call on your god! Maybe he will take notice of us, and we will not perish.'
>
> Then the sailors said to each other, "Come let us cast lots to find out who is responsible for this calamity". They cast lots and the lot fell on Jonah. (Jonah 1:4–7)

COMMENTS

The aftermath of Jonah's complaining is not that he then draws near to God. No, instead Jonah's complaining to God sours into disobedience. He resigns as God's prophet and, with wilful disobedience, leaves Zebulun and travels to Joppa to find a ship bound for Tarshish.

God has listened to Jonah's complaining back in Israel and has watched his disobedience all the way from Zebulun down to Joppa then out to sea. We are not told why God waited until Jonah was out on the open sea before He reacted to Jonah's disobedience. God could have disturbed his journey to Joppa just as Christ disturbed Saul's (Paul's) journey to Damascus. Ever since Genesis (Genesis 3:15), God has made plain that He has a reaction to disobedience and scripture is littered with examples of how and when He responds. In the case of Jonah, God begins to show his response to Jonah's disobedience when Jonah is at sea.

The phrase "the LORD sent a great wind" is put slightly differently in other translations. The New American and Revised Standard versions, and Laetsch, use the expression "the LORD hurled a great wind". The Revised English Bible says "the LORD let loose a hurricane" and the Jerusalem Version says "Yahweh unleashed a violent wind." The words "hurled", "unleashed" and "let loose" convey the force of the original Hebrew which is the same word used to describe Saul hurling a javelin at David (1 Samuel 20:33).

Since its creation by God, Nature is responsive to Him. God speaks to the great sea creature and it vomits out Jonah (Jonah 2:10). God hurls a wind and a tempest erupts. Jesus rebukes the wind and waves, and there is calm (Luke 8:24). Yet not all winds are sent or calmed by God. In Job 1:19 Satan delivers a strong wind that causes the death of all of Job's sons. In Acts 27 Paul is given anticipation from an angel that he will be delivered from a storm — but God does not say who sends the storm. This side of Eden; to discern the activity of God in Nature is no trifle. As an aside, it concerns me how often and confident some people are in their statements that God has acted. Knowledge and experience harnessed by His Spirit may yield insights, but abiding clarity is rare, at least that is my experience.

In the book of Job the wind delivered by Satan was part of his attempt to destroy all that was precious between God and Job. In the book of Jonah the wind was an agent to restore all that was necessary and precious between God and Jonah — obedience to God.

The phrase "the ship threatened to break up" also has special meaning.

In Hebrew it literally means "it (the ship) thought it would be broken in pieces". This animating device in Hebrew is used to display the power of the action — even the ship thought it faced ruin. God unleashes a violent storm. Its intensity is sufficient to frighten sailors supposedly experienced in life at sea, and even the ship thinks it will break up. Yet all this time the response of Jonah is deep sleep!

As Jonah sleeps on, the frightened sailors try to lighten the ship by throwing things overboard and each sailor cries to his god for help. In passing, it is perhaps worth noting, obedience to God has personal cost and other costs, but so does disobedience. The disobedience of Jonah cost these sailors their safety and probably much of their cargo. In one sense our disobedience is a private issue between God and ourselves but it also has a public dimension. Other people, and even Nature, can be harmed or disadvantaged by our disobedience.

The nationalities of the crew cannot be accurately discerned from the text, but those scholars who venture comment say they would mostly be Phoenician. Tarshish was a Phoenician colony. Israel had no merchant navy and mostly relied on Phoenician vessels. Even under the kingships of Solomon and Jehosaphat, when Israel briefly had a navy, the Phoenicians built and manned the ships.

Phoenicians were not monotheistic but worshipped a variety of gods. Their gods were often depicted as stern and demanding, constantly in need of pacification. In certain cases, worshippers even gave their children as sacrifices in order to restore the favour of the gods.

While the storm rages, Jonah snores; at least that is how the Septuagint translation puts it. The Hebrew word for Jonah's sleep implies unusually heavy sleep. It is the same word in noun form in Genesis 2:21 to describe the sleep of Adam (see Genesis 15:12; Judges 4:21 and Daniel 8:18 for other deep sleepers). The deepness of the sleep contrasts sharply with the wakeful distress of the sailors. As a literary device the deep sleep adds to the humour and novelty of the book. Nowhere does the text explain why he slept so deeply.

It could be that the combination of the shock of being asked to speak in Nineveh, the immense anger with God over possibly sparing judgement, the long journey down to Joppa, the emotion of farewelling Israel and explanations to the crew, in total extracted a heavy psychological and physical toll. He is now very tired. At last he can rest; he is on his way to truly show God that the end of the world is preferable to Nineveh. Although many commentators have similar explanations for Jonah's depth of sleep; some have very different explanations. For instance, Jerome thinks Jonah's sleep arose from his security of mind, his calmness and tranquillity. Marck supposes his sleep was deep as he knew by sleeping he would better escape the dangers of sea and air or the hand of God. Whatever the true reason for his sleep, it is probably more important to recognize that while he slept, God worked. God works in our waking and sleeping.

The severity of the storm quickly brings the sailors to a position where they know their own skilfulness as mariners is not sufficient to save them from perishing. They keep working, and each sailor cries to his god for help. Below deck the captain, perhaps while searching to see what other cargo should be cast off, discovers a sleeping Jonah. Waking Jonah, the captain makes the reasonable request that Jonah too should turn to his God for aid. But since his last complaining conversation with God, the main turning Jonah has been doing has been turning in his sleep and more particularly, turning away from God. Although not obvious in the text, when the captain spoke to Jonah, Jonah would have understood what was saying. Assuming, as is highly likely, that the ship and crew were mostly Phoenicians then the language spoken on board would have been Phoenician that is virtually pure Hebrew. Phoenician and Hebrew are like two dialects of the same language.

It is interesting that the ship's captain (in Hebrew, literally "the chief rope puller") orders Jonah in verse 6 to "arise" and "call" to his god. The same actions (even the same Hebrew words) are those originally requested by God to Jonah back in verse 2 of chapter 1, when Jonah is told to "arise" and "call" against Nineveh.

The nature of the storm and perhaps the nature of their gods convince the sailors someone on board has offended a god. To identify the person, they cast lots which was in Old Testament times a fairly widespread cultural practice. It was used as a means of guidance in apportioning territory, duties or blame and for making appointments. It was a divination tool regarded as being fairly reliable and would have credibility with Jonah and sailors alike. The lot fell on Jonah.

So they asked him, "Tell us, who is responsible for making all this trouble for us? What do you do? Where do you come from? What is your country? From what people are you?"

He answered, "I am a Hebrew and I worship the LORD, the God of heaven, who made the sea and the dry land."

This terrified them and they asked, "What have you done? (They knew he was running away from the LORD, because he had already told them so.)

The sea was getting rougher and rougher. So they asked him, "What should we do to you to make the sea calm down for us?"

"Pick me up and throw me into the sea," he replied, "and it will become calm. I know that it is my fault that this great storm has come upon you." (Jonah 1:8–12)

COMMENTS

Before the lot fell on Jonah, it seems from verse 10 that he had already told the sailors he was fleeing from the presence of God. Hence, I am surprised that the sailors did not earlier suspect Jonah to be the culprit given his recent dealings with a god and his resignation as that god's minister. It is clear from the sailors' responses in verses 8 and 10 that they had little knowledge of either Jonah or his God. Perhaps they thought the god from whom Jonah fled was like many other Phoenician gods, being localized. They may have viewed Jonah at sea as being sufficiently away from his god as to be outside the bounds of this god's power, and so Jonah might not be blameworthy. However, the casting of the lot seals the issue and the guilt of Jonah is revealed.

The sailors then fire questions at Jonah to discover the nature of his guilt and person. The sailors hear that he is a Hebrew, but more important, his god is altogether different from their many localized gods. According to Jonah, his God is "the God of heaven who made the sea and dry land." Well! Their situation was obvious. The sailors probably thought: here is a foolish passenger. Fancy trying to flee and cease being the servant of a god who made the sea and the dry land. No wonder this god is angry with him and no wonder the sea is uncharacteristically violent.

Even though, to his credit, Jonah has told the sailors truthful and lasting things about God; nonetheless, quite rightly, the sailors berate Jonah. Both Laetsch and the New American Standard Version translate the sailors' comments in verse 10 as: "How could you do it?"

Jonah figuratively waved goodbye to God back in Israel; now God waves hello even more furiously to Jonah — "The sea was getting rougher and rougher." It is as if God's anger, like the sea, is mounting. God has placed before Jonah a series of opportunities for Jonah to recognize his need to be God's servant rather than the servant of anger and disappointment; the servant of his own emotions and self-assessments. There has been a tempestuous storm to jolt Jonah from sleep. The captain has asked him: What do you mean by sleeping? Call upon your god! The lots have been cast and Jonah selected. He has been asked by crew members: What's your occupation? And, how could you do what you've done? On all these occasions and in various ways God has been providing Jonah with opportunities to think again, to remember, to be guided by God's Spirit and not his own self-righteous spirit. It is the same throughout history. God seeks out people. He wishes to gather them in His arms like a mother with her child. Remember the lukewarm Christians at Laodecia and Christ pounding on their door (Revelations 3). Every heard knock was an opportunity; a reproof and stimulation so that Christ and believer could be united. With great power God has been knocking on the door of Jonah's heart and mind.

The sailors ask Jonah what they need to do to ensure the sea will quieten. Jonah says they should cast him overboard. Plainly, Jonah sees his own death is warranted. Keil-Delitsch say that Jonah's knowledge of Mosaic law and his knowledge of God's dealings with His people would lead Jonah to conclude that severe yet just punishment should be applied to himself, and that death by drowning was appropriate. Allen says that Jonah's request to be thrown overboard was not Jonah's final solution to evade his mission to Nineveh nor was it a gallant sacrifice to save the sailors' lives, rather it was Jonah indicating his guilt before God, for he was willing to die because of his grave disobedience. However, Laetsch says Jonah did offer himself as the victim to be sacrificed in order to save the sailors. Feinberg agrees with Laetsch but also adds that Jonah considered himself worthy of death due to his disobedience. Thus, there is no consensus on the exact reasons for Jonah's request to be thrown overboard. Certainly, Jonah perceived it as necessary and his prayer in chapter 2 makes clear that he saw his casting into the sea as an act of God —

> You hurled me into the deep,
> into the very heart of the seas,
> and the currents swirled about me,
> all your waves and breakers swept over me. (Jonah 2:4)

Jonah's anticipation was to die by the hand of God, drowning in His waves and breakers.

At this point in the story of Jonah, fact or fiction, it is worth noting that we have been given more glimpses of the inner persons of the sailors than we have of Jonah. We have been told that they "were afraid"; they have "cried out" and been "terrified". By contrast we are not yet told Jonah's emotional state. So far, the text makes plain that Jonah was industrious, eager and seemingly unafraid, even to the point of asking others, cultural strangers, to do things that he knows will lead to his death. This death is not martyrdom. It is, in Jonah's eyes, a deserved and just judgement, and so perhaps no great emotion is recorded of him, even at this awful point when facing death.

> Instead, the men did their best to row back to land. But they could not, for the sea grew wilder than before. Then they cried to the LORD, "O LORD, please do not let us die for taking this man's life. Do not hold us accountable for killing an innocent man, for you, O LORD, have done as you pleased." Then they took Jonah and threw him overboard, and the raging sea grew calm. At this the men greatly feared the LORD, and they offered a

sacrifice to the LORD and made vows to him. But the LORD provided a great fish to swallow Jonah, and Jonah was inside the fish three days and three nights. (Jonah 1:13–16)

COMMENTS

The sailors respond to Jonah's statement that he should be thrown overboard by spending much of their last energies trying to save his life rather than end it. They row hard. The Hebrew words mean literally "to dig through the waves".

The ships to Tarshish were large ships with a deck, a single large square sail and often a double bank of thirty to sixty oars used mostly when becalmed. In Old Testament times the routes of voyages often followed coastlines, as seems to be the case here, with the sailors hoping to land the ship by rowing hard and long. However, with worsening seas and tired bodies they realize they have no energy left to save either Jonah or the ship by rowing further. They cry to God and in their prayer to God they ask Him not to be vengeful toward them for delivering Jonah into the sea. They do not want to be seen by this God as murderers. In effect they say that God has already condemned Jonah in the casting of the lot, or as the King James Version says, "for Thou, O LORD, hast done as it pleased Thee". The phrase "hast done as it pleased Thee" should not be interpreted as meaning God has derived pleasure in the form of humour or gaiety from the event, for elsewhere God says "For I have no pleasure in the death of him that dieth, saith the Lord God." (Ezekiel 18:32a, KJV). Rather the phrase should be viewed in the sense of God being satisfied (pleased) to carry out His will which ultimately is for Jonah to respond to Him as His servant.

After Jonah is tossed overboard, the sea ceases its raging. Then all the mariners fear God exceedingly, offering Him a sacrifice and making vows. What the mariners use to offer a sacrifice is not mentioned; but according to Smith (2011) it may have been animals that formed part of the cargo.

Although the form of the sailors worshipping is probably the same as they would use to their Phoenician gods, nonetheless they are worshipping God. I note this because it is quite possible to have many different culturally-influenced outward forms of worship, yet still God can be worshipped, as long as the activity is genuine and heart-felt in praise of Him. True worship requires honest engagement, not the pretence of giving honour; as Isaiah 29:13 states:

The Lord says:

"These people come near to me with their mouth and honour me with their lips, but their hearts are far from me. Their worship of me is based on merely human rules they have been taught."

Hence, in any period of history, when the outward nature of worship is codified and regulated, there is a risk of giving prominence to the outward display rather than registering the more important issue of the inward nature of worship to honour and praise God. The rigour, ritual or ingredients of worship can become ends in themselves. However, contrarily and at best, these same things can also facilitate the true worship of God.

The sailors have seen the purity and power of God at work and they have heard about God from Jonah's dying testimony. God's actions towards Jonah and the mariners are often repeated in history, insofar as God brings people to the end of their abilities or experiences, when self-reliance is no longer a comfortable or viable option. In these circumstances, some people will think on Him or remember and turn to Him. When rowing hard through the seas of life seemingly delivers nought and circumstances appear to conspire against us, stripping us of any sense of control over our destiny, then sometimes people turn to God with the wish that He be real, responsive and not condemnatory.

There are wonderful verses in the Psalms to encourage us to not leave our interactions with God only to the desperate or devastating moments of life when self-reliance is so obviously no longer sufficient comfort. In Psalm 39 the psalmist asks of God to "Show me, O Lord, my life's end and the number of my days: let me know how fleeting is my life." (Psalm 39:4). To meditate on our death and the brevity of our lives is to lift our gaze from the immediacy of events and thereby see our true frailty and need of God. In Psalm 127:1 we read that "Unless the Lord builds the house, the workers have laboured in vain." Again the implication is the need to rely on and interact with God in our walk with Him.

It is a sad reflection that He who created heaven and earth is not asked to do more building in all parts of our lives, rather than being occasionally called in as the emergency plumber.

Note that God provides the great fish not to kill or drown Jonah, but to swallow him, to provide Jonah with a physical sanctum in which remembrance is made possible. The prayer of Jonah which forms the bulk of chapter 2 contains no direct reference at all to the great fish. In fact, reference to the great fish occurs in only two verses in the book of Jonah (Jonah 1:17 and Jonah 2:10) and on both occasions the fish is subject to God's actions. God *provided* the great fish (Jonah 1:17) to swallow Jonah and God *commanded* the great fish and it vomited Jonah on to dry land (Jonah 2:10). Although mentioned only twice in the entire book, nonetheless the great fish often is given centre-stage in illustrations and descriptions of the book and unfortunately even receives prominence in some teachings of the book.

As we leave chapter 1, we can further note two things. Firstly, the mariners vowed vows when they saw the work of God. By contrast, back in Israel Jonah relinquished his prophetic vows when he foresaw the work of God. Secondly, it is unfortunate that the term being *"a Jonah"* has entered common parlance with the inference that the person brings misfortune. In fact, because of the presence of Jonah, the mariners came to know and worship God which can never rightly be called a misfortune. Because of all that the book of Jonah tells us, it is unfair that so many people link his name solely to a harbinger of disaster; *"a Jonah"*.

A last observation that relates to the sovereignty of God is that even Jonah's disobedience forms part of the pathway for the mariners to honour God. This is not to justify Jonah's disobedience, but rather to show that a man's sinfulness will not prevent the power and revelation of God being displayed such that others come to worship Him.

JONAH CHAPTER TWO

From inside the fish Jonah prayed to the LORD his God
He said:
"In my distress I called to the LORD,
and he answered me.
From the depths of the grave
I called for help,
and you listened to my cry.
You hurled me into the deep,
into the very heart of the seas,
and the currents swirled about me;
all your waves and breakers swept over me.
I said, ' I have been banished from your sight;
yet I will look again towards your holy temple.'
The engulfing waters threatened me,
the deep surrounded me;
seaweed was wrapped around my head.
To the roots of the mountains I sank down;
the earth beneath barred me in forever.
But you brought my life up from the pit,
O LORD my God.
"When my life was ebbing away,
I remembered you, LORD,
and my prayer rose to you,
to your holy temple.
"Those who cling to worthless idols
forfeit the grace that could be theirs.

But I, with a song of thanksgiving, will sacrifice to you.
What I have vowed I will make good.
Salvation comes from the LORD."

And the LORD commanded the fish, and it vomited
Jonah on to dry land. (Jonah 2:1–11)

COMMENTS

Having earlier discussed the issues surrounding the great fish, all I will add here is that the fish is part of God's deliverance of Jonah from suffering and drowning in the sea. Jonah's stay in this fish is the only sign Christ gives of Himself to those who sought a sign as to His nature and authenticity — "Christ died and returned to life so that he might be the Lord of both the dead and the living." (Romans 14:9). This sign was also to remind his generation that He was the fulfilment of scripture and that by remembering such scripture, clarity about the nature and purpose of Christ would be cemented.

The three days and three nights mentioned in verse 1 does not necessarily equal seventy-two hours. The Hebrew convention is that part of a day equals a day and similarly for a night. According to Keil-Delitsch, the time period mentioned would mean that Jonah was vomited up on the third day after he had been swallowed. The number three usually is associated with certain of God's mighty acts (see Luke 13:32; Exodus 19:11; Hosea 6:2).

In this fish Jonah offers a prayer of thanksgiving to God for having been delivered from death and error. Given the nature of this prayer, many scholars wonder if this prayer was ever part of the original narrative and label it an interpolation by some copyist to explain God's decision to save Jonah. Other scholars see the prayer as originally present. Harrison says, for example, "While the psalm is of a different character from the remainder of the prophecy, there is insufficient evidence to show that it has actually been interpolated by a later hand." The text of Jonah 2 verse 1 indicates that Jonah did pray while in the fish's belly, but whether or not this is the actual prayer of Jonah is not certain. Laetsch is more definite and I have much sympathy for his view. He says, "The thoughts and emotions recorded in Jonah's prayer were those that actually passed through his mind during his imprisonment, and he may have given expression to some of them in the very words recorded. The final form of great poetical perfection and logical sequence found in chapter 2 was composed by him after his deliverance." Mind you, such views assume this prayer is history rather than the creative fiction of the writer of the book of Jonah.

Although the opening verse in chapter 2 reveals that Jonah prayed while inside the great fish, this was not the only time and place he prayed. Verses 3 to 7 make plain that as he was drowning, Jonah prayed. "....all your waves and breakers swept over me. I said, 'I have been banished from your sight" (Jonah 2:3–4) and later "When my life was ebbing away, I remembered you, Lord" (Jonah 2:7). Hence, in his panic and distress he importantly prayed to God, noting what He did and remembering Him.

The prayer recorded in chapter 2 is overall a prayer of thanksgiving, although the prayer begins with outlining his distress and affliction. As observed before, God sometimes uses such circumstances so that people turn to Him. In the book of Hosea a poignant portion describes how the Valley of Achor (misfortune or troubling) is a door of hope (Hosea 2:5b–15). Similarly, Paul outlines the sequence whereby "we know that suffering produces perseverance, perseverance, character; and character, hope." (Romans 5:3–4). For many of us, when earthly help is inadequate or evanescent, there is opportunity to draw near to God. It is a reality for many in distress that they call to God. In fact, it's part of common parlance: "God help us."

It's worth noting the change in grammar within verse 2, whereby Jonah initially speaks of God in the third person but then speaks of God with the familiar term 'you' or 'thou'. Jonah says: "In my distress I called to the Lord and he answered me. From the depths of the grave I called for help, and *You* listened to my cry." At the start of the verse Jonah was speaking about God in the third person just as he had been doing so before on the ship (see Jonah 1:9). However, the magnitude of Jonah's precarious situation led him to not just speak about God, but to speak *to* Him. The adversity experienced by Jonah led to intimacy, to real interaction with God.

This is an important observation. Affliction brought by God can serve

His purposes. It can serve to demonstrate His salvation and bring us to worship Him. It is important, however, to note that affliction, of itself, is neither efficacious nor desirable. To be poor, afflicted and bruised is not a state that warrants commendation. Rather it is the calling to God, the remembering of Him, created by the awareness of our status before God that is the desirable outcome. That a Valley of Achor (misfortune or troubling) is part of the path and door to hope is a work of God for the purpose of our salvation.

In the book of Samuel, Hannah experienced her personal Valley of Achor; the long awful pain of childlessness. She shared her pain with God and He remembered her, resulting in her falling pregnant with Samuel (1 Samuel 1:19). Her prayer of thankfulness records the power and might of God, how He "lifts the needy from the ash heap" (1 Samuel 2:8) and that the Lord "brings down to the grave and raises up" (1 Samuel 2:6). Jonah is such an example of being brought down to the grave and being raised up. Such are the words in part of Jonah's prayer:

> To the roots of the mountains I sank down;
> the earth beneath barred me in forever.
> But you brought my life up from the pit,
> O LORD my God. (Jonah 2:6)

In verse 3 is a phrase that is variously translated as "belly of the nether-world" or "belly of Sheol" or "womb of hell" or "depths of the grave". Some commentators, of whom Jerome is one, say that this phrase is only referring to the belly of the fish. Others say the phrase is a poetical expression used to denote the danger of death. A few others suppose it implies Jonah was actually brought to the very gates of hell; because of the link between hades and Sheol. From the wording of the text there appears little support for the first view that the phrase only refers to the fish's belly. My inclination is to agree with those saying the expression refers to Jonah being at death's door, rather than actually speaking at hell's gates.

Finally, near death, Jonah speaks not about God, as he did when with the sailors, but rather *to* God. The Authorized Version draws attention to this by using the word *thou*. In the face of death, intimacy returns; "thou heardest my voice." There can be intimacy near death; Daniel in the lions' pit, Stephen being stoned and Jesus in the garden at Gethsemane. And in such intimacy God hears.

The prayers of all saints are preserved like incense which ascends to God (Revelation 5:8 and 8:3). Remember the comment about Cornelius' prayers: "Your prayers and gifts to the poor have come up as a remembrance before God" (Acts 10:4b). Our genuine and mindful prayers are welcomed and given value and importance by God. That is not to say God always says yes to our pleadings — Paul, for one, learned that concerning his infirmity.

Another textual difficulty in chapter 2 concerns the latter half of verse 4. In the Jerusalem version (verse 5), the Revised Standard version and the Revised English Bible the verse reads as if Jonah despairs of seeing God's temple again. For example, the Revised Standard Version says;

> Then I said, "I am cast out from thy presence;
> how shall I again look upon thy holy temple?"

However, in Keil-Delitzsch, the Authorized, the New American Standard, and New International versions and in recent translations by Laetsch and Allen, the opposite view emerges that Jonah was confident that he would see the temple. For example, the New International version says;

> I said, "I have been banished from your sight;
> yet I will look again towards your holy temple."

What is the correct translation all hinges on a Hebrew word which according to some manuscript sources can be translated to mean "how", while other manuscript sources imply the word means "but" or "yet" or "surely". Hence, until further scholastic research uncovers clarifying evidence, the issue is unresolved. It is true that whichever translation is taken affects the mood of the prayer at this point. However, the overall nature of the prayer as praise and thanksgiving remains unaffected whichever translation is followed.

The words used in verses 5 and 6 illustrate Jonah's drowning and also the geographical thinking of the time. It was believed that the earth rested or floated on a subterranean ocean and the roots of the mountains went down into this sea. Jonah while drowning was being wrapped around by sea-weed and feeling that the gates of earth were closed to him. He was imprisoned behind sea-bars and was destined to die. Yet from death by drowning God saves him.

The commentator Barnes makes the observation that "God sent the fish to deliver him". This is an important point not to gloss over. When re-telling the story of Jonah it is a facile error to think that because God punishes wrong-doing that Jonah's punishment was to be swallowed by the great fish. I can almost hear a children's Sunday school teacher saying: "Jonah was naughty so he was thrown overboard and was swallowed by a whale!"; yet the purpose of the great fish was to be a means of salvation, not punishment!

The last words in Jonah's prayer in verse 9 reveal a theme begun in Genesis 3:15, and which is then sprinkled across scripture; namely that "Salvation comes from the LORD." God's salvation is a common theme in scripture. Other pithy statements about the salvation of God are in Psalm 30:2–3 and 2 Corinthians 1:8b–10 which says —

> We despaired even of life. Indeed, in our hearts we felt
> the sentence of death. But this happened that we might
> not rely on ourselves but on God, who raises the dead.
> He has delivered us...

Beginning to rely on God and not himself is what Jonah did when he remembered God.

> When my life was ebbing away,
> I remembered you, LORD,
> and my prayer rose to you,
> to your holy temple. (Jonah 2:7)

God's activity; deliberate, powerful and persistent, has brought Jonah to the point of remembrance; his gateway to true comfort. This lesson which Jonah illustrates is important: our salvation is God's province and our role is simply to place reliance in Him, to remember Him. Jonah's remembrance of God was his pathway to security yet it was God who drew near to Jonah to welcome him into His book of life.

In reflection; many of us may live in situations or cultures where the immediacy of daily tasks or the flow of unquestioned habit squeezes out opportunity for remembrance of God. Yet remembrance of God is deep security. That is not to say that the world or nature or habits are unimportant or are at heart a distraction. No, for in them can be the experience of God, His wonder and mystery. However, there is a risk that the lure of being diligent and successful in daily life squeezes out remembrance and worship of God.

To remember Him is to create and visit the store in our hearts and minds of our knowledge, memories and experiences of Him and His ways. To be open to the Spirit of God and not just the spirit of the world is to build from the bedrock of remembrance of Him. In the words of the Revised English Bible's translation of Jonah 2:9: "Those who cling to false gods may abandon their loyalty." When we live far from our bedrock then the lure of self-congratulation, wealth, position, prowess and judgement of others soon sidles up in various guises to different degrees to push aside remembrance of Him. Or self-absorption in dread, pessimism, loneliness or self-loathing can also steer us away from God. How simple, how difficult it can be to remember God.

And what if we lose the faculty of remembrance? While we can remember, we should enjoy the privilege. But when we can't, then our bedrock (though we may not know it) remains God's love for us which is not conditional on our mental or emotional prowess. As Paul says: ".... neither the present nor the future, nor any powers, neither height nor depth, nor anything else in all creation, will be able to separate us from the love of God...." (Romans 8: 38b–39). The mentally ill or incapacitated are loved by God; "a bruised reed he will not break and a smouldering wick he will not snuff out" (Isaiah 42:3).

Jonah knew that salvation comes from God, a statement often repeated in scripture (see Psalm 3:8; Psalm 34:18; Acts 4:12; Acts 2:21; John 3:17). Ever since Eden, God's unswerving commitment to salvation is evident (Genesis 3:15b). Hence, to stand in the way of, or attempt to impede, God's work of salvation is a very, very dangerous stance. Despite

Jonah's disobedience and complaining to God, nonetheless God's work of salvation occurs.

At the close of Jonah's prayer we find him worshipping God. Like the mariners, Jonah's experience of God leads to worship and vows.

> But I, with a song of thanksgiving,
> will sacrifice to you.
> What I have vowed I will make good.
> Salvation comes from the LORD. (Jonah 2:9)

The vows that Jonah will make good are almost certainly his prophetic vows to serve God.

The last verse in chapter 2 where God speaks to the fish and it vomits out Jonah onto the dry land is indicative of God's authority and power over Nature and its responsiveness to Him. Those who believe the fish to be a whale have little difficulty believing the historicity of this verse, given the frequency with which whales, particularly pods of whales, beach themselves. Those who see the event as fiction would acknowledge how it makes the story of Jonah so easily memorable.

Where Jonah is beached is not stated in the text, yet Josephus suggests it was on the coast of the Euxine Sea (Black Sea), bordering Turkey. Keil-Delitzsch, on the other hand, say it was, of course, the coast of Palestine. The point to note, however, is that wherever Jonah was beached was far from Nineveh. The Palestine and Euxine coastlines each lay over 800 kilometres from Nineveh.

The journey to Nineveh would take weeks, be arduous and possibly at times would be dangerous. The nature of such a journey should be remembered. A quick reading of the text of Jonah may overlook this journey and make Jonah's behaviour in chapter 4 seem impetuous and his commitment to God in chapter 2 brief and superficial. Brief though the book of Jonah may be does not mean that the experiences written about concerning him were also brief. Whether fact or fiction his journeys were long and demanding.

An often under-stated feature of the book of Jonah is how much prominence is given to prayer. Over a sixth of the book is devoted to prayer; the prayer chiefly of thanksgiving in chapter 2 and the prayer of complaint in chapter 4. The facility with which Jonah prays says much about his confidence in God and the maturity and longevity of his relationship with God. Jonah is not like the New Testament disciples who sought to be taught how to pray (Luke 11:1). Prayer was for Jonah already a confidence, an enabled practised behaviour. Jonah shares his pain, his sorrow, his thankfulness, his knowledge, his anger, his confidence, his desires with God. We are given the privilege as a reader to listen to his most intimate conversations with God.

Jonah, this bruised reed (Isaiah 42:3), whenever prayerful, receives careful response from God. Jonah calls to God; God answers (Jonah 2:2). Jonah calls out to God, God listens (Jonah 2:2). Jonah complains to God (Jonah 2:2) and God replies to his complaint (Jonah 2:4). Jonah's prayer is so valued by God that it is heard in the courts of heaven (Jonah 2:7). The same applies to us. Our prayer is heard from heaven (2 Chronicles 7:14); Christ teaches us to pray to our Father in heaven. Solomon's prayer plainly says: "Hear from heaven, Your dwelling-place; and when You hear, forgive." (2 Chronicles 6:21). And though in heaven, God is responsive. "The Lord is near to all who call on Him, to all who call on Him in truth." (Psalm 145:18).

JONAH CHAPTER THREE

Then the word of the LORD came to Jonah a second time:

> "Go to the great city of Nineveh and proclaim to it the message I give you."

> Jonah obeyed the word of the LORD and went to Nineveh. Now Nineveh was a very large city; it took three days to go all through it.

> Jonah started into the city a distance of a day's journey, and he proclaimed:

> "Forty more days and Nineveh shall be destroyed."
> (Jonah 3:1–4)

COMMENTS

God again commands Jonah to go to Nineveh with His words, and this time Jonah obeys. Nothing is said of the danger or tiresomeness of Jonah's journey to Nineveh. Nothing is said of the personal difficulty he would experience as a stranger alone in a large city. Nineveh is still the same city with its rapacious violence; yet there is no mention of complaint from Jonah.

Jonah responded to the word of the LORD; not to his own assessments and misgivings. For those who honour obedience to God, this is Jonah at his best. But it is also, in a way, Jonah being vulnerable; for he is required to head to a place he otherwise would not choose to visit. It is a city not renowned for the provision of safety to strangers and so has the potential to offer frustration, danger and bewilderment. Remember, the Jonah in 2 Kings 14:25 was from Gath Hepher, a small country town. He now faces the bustle, hazards and complexity of a large city.

It seems that things that might otherwise have cluttered his thinking or unhelpfully swayed his emotions have faded. In this moment he has singularly remembered and acted upon God's beckoning. For those who believe in and are fashioned by the servitude of Christ (Isaiah 49: 5–6) then like Jonah, at their best these folk are God's servants—listening to and being obedient to Him.

In giving Jonah yet another opportunity to be His servant, God is also enlivening His relationship with Jonah by giving him a chance to respond rightly. Something similar applies on the human plane of relationships where, for a relationship to grow, there must be opportunities for reflection, and if possible, opportunities for response.

When Jonah comes to Nineveh, he arrives at a great city of three day's journey. The phrase "three day's journey", used in several translations, is a measure of diameter rather than circumference, and likely included in the measure are Nineveh's satellite towns. In Genesis 10:11–12 Nineveh and its satellite towns of Calah, Rehoboth-ir and Resen together are called the great city. The traverse of this great city would take a journey of three days, even though the inner city of Nineveh only had a circumference of about twelve kilometres.

Jonah's message to the people of Nineveh was pithy and powerful. Starkly, the word translated as "destroyed" or "overthrown" means to utterly destroy even to the foundations. It is the same word used in describing the annihilation of Sodom and Gomorrah (Genesis 19:21, 25, 29). And what is the significance of the forty days? The New Bible Dictionary says the number forty is associated with almost each new development in the history of God's mighty acts, especially of salvation. For example, the number forty applies to aspects of the great flood in Noah's time, Israel's redemption from Egypt, Elijah and the prophetic era, the advent of Christ and the birth of the Church. Leslie Allen says the forty day period may represent a period of testing and waiting, such as Christ's forty days in the wilderness and Israel's forty years in the desert.

Both these views have merit for the entire destruction of Nineveh would be a mighty act of God, and given God's response in verse 10 of this chapter, the forty days could be seen as a period of remorseful waiting.

I find it hard to imagine what it would have been like for Jonah to be in Nineveh; armed with a message of awful judgment yet, as far as we know, being alone. His language, Hebrew, probably was not well known in Nineveh which may have meant Jonah needed to speak in Aramaic, the language of trade. He would have been surrounded by a geographical terrain, a city, its people and language; almost certainly all new to him. He was from a small village in Zebulun, yet now was thrust into the limelight of a vast city.

I know how uncomfortable it can be to be alone and a stranger in a city in a foreign country surrounded by a language you do not comprehend. I've experienced that discomfort; I'm no adventurer. I do not know, however, what it is like to be in such a city to preach a message of judgment that the people are not expecting nor would want to hear. That Jonah is obedient to speak and capable to speak in ways that even reach the king of Nineveh I find remarkable.

I can understand why Moses was reticent (Exodus 4:13). I can understand why Martin Niemöller after personally experiencing the evil of the Third Reich, said:

> First they came for the Communists, but I was not a Communist so I did not speak out. Then they came for the Socialists and the Trade Unionists, but I was neither, so I did not speak out. Then they came for the Jews, but I was not a Jew so I did not speak out. And when they came for me, there was no one left to speak out for me.[7]

By contrast to one even as great as Moses, Jonah was, despite his flaws, not timid. In many ways he is an impressive, passionate person, with great energy and courage. Perhaps we too often misjudge him and

---

[7] The origins of this quote have been traced to a speech given by Niemöller on January 6, 1946, to the representatives of the Confessing Church in Frankfurt.

linger too long on his frailties. At times he rightly wears the mantle of a proper prophet; a beacon of obedience and bravery.

> The Ninevites believed God. They ordered a public fast, and put on sackcloth, from the greatest of them to the least of them.
>
> When the news reached the king of Nineveh, he rose from his throne, took off his royal robes, covered himself with sackcloth and sat down in the dust.
>
> Then he issued a proclamation in Nineveh:
>
> "By the decree of the king and his nobles;
> Do not let any man or beast, herd or flock,
> taste anything; do not let them eat or drink.
> But let man and beast be covered with sackcloth.
> Let everyone call urgently on God.
> Let them give up their evil ways and their violence.
> Who knows? God may yet relent and with compassion turn from his fierce anger so that we will not perish."
>
> When God saw what they did and how they turned from their evil ways, he had compassion and did not bring upon them the destruction he had threatened. (Jonah 3:5–10)

COMMENTS

The staggering and almost unimaginable response to Jonah's preaching is that the people of Nineveh believed God. It may seem a small thing but though Jonah has been doing all the talking, it is *God* whom the people believe. Jonah speaks but the people hear God. It is one thing to consider as plausible or credible what someone says; it is another thing, however, to discern that the words are God's words. Jonah was not dismissed as a bitter foreigner or as bizarre entertainment. His words were seen to be

God's words, or at least that's what the writer of the book would have us believe.

When you consider how many inhabitants there were in Nineveh, at least 120,000 children (Jonah 4:11), and how many foreign visitors must have passed through its gates; it is surprising and seemingly improbable that the words of a single visitor, Jonah, could firstly be heard above the din and multitude of all other local and foreign voices. Additionally and practically, how did Jonah manage to speak to sufficient inhabitants for his message to then be so widely disseminated that even the king became aware of his message?

Why did the Ninevites believe God? Why did Nineveh repent? The exact answer remains a mystery but various commentators offer suggestions. Perowne, for example, considers their oriental minds aided Jonah's task and so Perowne says "To an oriental mind, the simple oft-repeated announcement (by Jonah) might (have been) more startling than a laboured address." In other words, the pithy repetition was persuasive. Not knowing, however, how an oriental mind differs from any other mind, I'm not competent to assess the merits of Perowne's view.

Other commentators suggest the circumstances around the time of Jonah's appearance would have conditioned the Ninevites to take seriously Jonah's message. Explaining further; scholars who see Jonah as a person in history consider his trip to Nineveh occurred somewhere in the first half of the eighth century BC. The first half of that century was a period of setbacks for Assyria. It found itself on the defensive having lost some of its territory to its north-eastern enemy Urartu. Its vassal states seeing Assyria's power weakened, also revolted such that Assyria was for a short time forced back to its homelands. This decline in Assyria's power was during the period in which Israel, as Jonah had prophesied, increased its territory.

To worsen matters there was a severe plague in Nineveh in 765 BC and yet another one six years later. To cap all this, there was the dreadful omen, for a superstitious people, of a total eclipse of the sun in 763 BC. Several commentators argue that it was during this troubling time for Nineveh when Jonah arrived. Yet Nineveh still had its reputation and behaviour of malice and brutality and, in a matter of decades, Assyria rose to greater heights of power and territorial conquest.

Another explanation of Nineveh's readiness to accept the veracity of Jonah's words comes from a link between the city's sign and Jonah's recent experience with the great fish. The Sumerian ideogram for the word "Nineveh" was a sign showing a fish enclosed in a tomb or womb. Located adjacent to the Tigris river, Nineveh relied on fish from the river. If the Ninevites knew of Jonah's entombment then they might see their city, the fish in the womb, linked to Jonah, the fish in the whale's womb. The similarities between Jonah and their city would make a superstitious people, as the Ninevites apparently were, think seriously about what Jonah said. Some commentators go as far to suggest that Jonah would still have a bleached skin from the great fish's stomach juices which would support his story of coming from the fish. However, unless there was permanent damage to his skin, the journey to Nineveh should have provided time for his skin to recover. Nonetheless, it does appear from Luke 11:30 that somehow Jonah was a sign to the Ninevites:

> For as Jonah became a sign to the men of Nineveh,
> so will the son of man be to this generation. (Luke 11:30)

There is also a comment that there was a local saying in Nineveh that their goddess Ishtar would one day send a messenger. Certainly, Jonah was a messenger but the response of the people was to see Jonah as God's messenger and not a messenger from Ishtar.

Whatever the rationale for the response of the Ninevites, it is worth noting that they are an example of God's declaration via the prophet Isaiah where He says: "I revealed myself to those who did not ask for me; I was found by those who did not seek me. To a nation that did not call on my name, I said, 'Here am I, here am I.'" (Isaiah 65:1). However unlikely, however improbable, God used a single person, Jonah, speaking His words and enabled an entire city, in a land distant from Israel, to hear and believe Him.

In responding to God, the people of Nineveh needed to face-up to His words of condemnation. These words of judgment were probably the first publicly heard words about God for many Ninevites. And the words informed the Ninevites that God was a powerful judge able to bring destruction and ruin. The message that God is our judge and that His judgments can bring ruin is not a message often heard in many Christian circles. Many would rather dwell on God as the loving, forgiving Father and shepherd. Yet it should be remembered that God is our judge and that sometimes He first comes to folk as He did at Nineveh as their judge. Centuries later Paul writes "For we will all stand before God's judgment seat ... each of us will give an account of himself to God." (Romans 14:10b, 12).

In verses 5 to 8 we read of the people's and the king's response to God which not only illustrates their remorse but also their culture. Wearing sackcloth, sitting in the dust or ashes and fasting were eastern modes of behaviour. Such practices accompanied feelings of grief, humiliation or sorrow. They were the outward signs of inner changes, although like any outward signs they could also be cheapened by conformity and pretence. In the case of Nineveh, if their repentance was an historical fact, then it appears to have been brief for they returned to violence, prompting their decimation as Nahum predicted. A relevant comment on the brevity of their repentance comes from Hugh Martin who observes that fear was a great and leading element in their response to God and that fear is the least noble of the elements that produce or lead to true repentance.

The treatment of animals in verses 7 and 8 is again a practice that was common among peoples like the Ninevites in that era. For example, the Persians clipped the manes of their horses and mules when their commander Masistios died. Another example is found in the apocryphal book of Judith 4:10. The Jewish commentator Metsudath David says the treatment of the animals is not because the animals too needed forgiveness, but that the withholding of food from them would be an added grief and penance for their owners.

Many of us may reside in cities and in countries where agriculture forms a small share of national employment or national economic wealth. Our societies are not agrarian yet the Assyrian Empire was an agrarian society. Control of productive agricultural land was an essential component of revenue generation, and agricultural produce from farms was taxed (Postgate 1979). The majority of land under Assyrian control was owned by the royal household (Bedford 2005). However, in order to mitigate the burden and expense of royal administration, tracts of the royal lands were allocated to high-ranking administrative officials to manage for their personal gain, on condition of providing the royal household with a share of the yields (Radner 2000). The fact that treatment of animals featured in the Ninevites' response is consistent with the agrarian nature of their economy and society.

The last phrase in verse eight makes plain the nature of Nineveh. Leslie Allen's translation is "Everyone is to turn from his wicked ways and meddling in violence." Laetsch expresses it as "Let them turn, each one, from his wicked way and from the violence they are committing." Even though Nineveh feasted on violence, the king's decree makes clear that he at least knew that such violence was wrong and unacceptable to God.

The Ninevites had been great helpers, helping themselves to as much gain as they could. They had trampled, massacred and bullied their way to richness. But before God they were helpless and poverty-stricken. Now they knew that their might, ferocity and riches would not protect them from God's judgment. What they did was to look to God, to rely on His mercy.

At this stage, uncomfortable though it may be, it is perhaps pertinent to ask who or what do we look to for security. Is our security the perishables of wealth, home, status, personal relationships, occupation or abilities? Or are we as the Ninevites who would "Look unto me and be ye saved" (Isaiah 45:22).

The marvellous and almost baffling response of God to the Ninevites, when He sees their contrition, is to suspend His judgment. Why does God do it? — Because He is a loving and gracious God and the Ninevites for once sought to depend on His mercy and not on their skilfulness and might. Just as Jonah looked to God and remembered Him so the Ninevites looked to God that He may turn and relent and withdraw His burning anger.

JONAH CHAPTER FOUR

But Jonah was greatly displeased and became angry. He prayed to the LORD, "O LORD, is this not what I said when I was still at home? That is why I was so quick to flee to Tarshish. I knew that you are a gracious and compassionate God, slow to anger and abounding in love, a God who relents from sending calamity. Now, O LORD, take away my life, for it is better for me to die than to live."

But the LORD replied, "Have you any right to be angry?"

Jonah went out and sat down at a place east of the city. There he made himself a shelter, sat in its shade and waited to see what would happen to the city. Then the LORD God provided a vine and made it grow up over Jonah to give shade for his head to ease his discomfort, and Jonah was very happy about the vine. But at dawn the next day God provided a worm, which chewed the vine so that it withered. When the sun rose, God provided a scorching east wind, and the sun blazed on Jonah's head so that he grew faint. He wanted to die, and said, "It would be better for me to die than to live."

But God said to Jonah, "Do you have a right to be angry about the vine?"

"I do," he said. "I am angry enough to die."

But the LORD said, "You have been concerned about this vine, though you did not tend it or make it grow. It sprang up overnight and died overnight. But Nineveh has more than a hundred and twenty thousand people who cannot tell their right hand from their left, and many cattle as well. Should I not be concerned about that great city?" (Jonah 4:1–11)

COMMENTS

Like the first chapter this last chapter is charged with action and emotion and, as has been the case throughout the book, we are given the privilege by the book's writer to look upon the private interchange between God and Jonah.

God has not destroyed Nineveh. He has looked with compassion upon Nineveh and has not left a single mark of His anger upon them, their animals or houses. But Jonah is furious. There is no compassion in him. His anticipations back in Israel boil again to the surface. The Hebrew word that describes Jonah's anger in verse 1 means to be like a metal heated to the point of being white hot. Laetsch in his translation says "Jonah burnt with anger."

However, the magnitude of his anger was no justification for his disapproval of God's mercy. Being faithful to his feelings in this case was not consistent with being faithful to God. For us, the Spirit of God should be our guide and teacher, not the spirit of the occasion or the emotion of the moment. Being a slave to emotion, to the whim or gigantic emotion of the moment, is not being a slave to God. However, having said that does not mean that emotion is improper, something to hide or stifle. God made us to experience emotion. My point is simply that our emotions should accompany our walk with God but not take the reins. Those who walk with God need not fear or serve emotion; they will be free to feel. And how those feelings are expressed will depend on the place, the setting, the culture, the family mores and the person's personality.

Earlier discussions in this devotional study canvassed the reasons for Jonah's anger. In a nutshell, Jonah's assessment was simple. Bad behaviour, especially by Israel's enemy, deserved a bad end. That God would delay or renege on justifiable destruction was intolerable. As T.J. Carlisle[8] says poetically:

> By heart he has learned –
> with what heart he had –
> devotedly and meticulously
> the eternal words.
> He could recite them
> without even thinking
> religiously exact
> and letter perfect,
> gracious, merciful
> slow to anger, abounding in steadfast love
> repenting of evil
> And now
> the blow:
> God genuinely meant it
> word for word
> What a pity !

God's initial response to Jonah is to ask him a question. In Hebrew the question is only three words. Given the depth of Jonah's emotion, the brevity and form of God's response may seem surprising. The English translations of God's response include "Have you any right to be angry?" or "Is it good for you to be angry?" or "Do you have good reason to be angry?" A similar question is asked again in verse 9. God seems to be asking Jonah to see his anger in perspective, rather than be consumed and directed by it. By asking Jonah a question, God is encouraging Jonah to think, rather than continue being driven solely by his emotion. It is God's plea for Jonah to exercise his mind not just his heart; to be sane,

---

[8] Reprinted with permission from the publisher, Wm. B. Eermans Publishing Company; all rights reserved.

to re-establish within himself a perspective on what is right and wrong, what is precious and what is veneer, what is worthy of anger and what is not.

But Jonah walked to the east side of Nineveh, perhaps simply because he entered the city from the west or for a purpose; as some say east is the direction from which God's judgment sometimes came in the Old Testament. He built himself a humpy out of branches as was the usual habit of shepherds watching their sheep. Jonah sat as the shepherd of Nineveh, watching over them, but preferring to lead them to the slaughter rather than any pastures. He waited more as a vulture than a dove, his name's meaning, wanting to see if God came to His senses and levelled the city.

An inadequate and light-hearted read of the book of Jonah would suggest that Jonah's life was plagued with inactivity. He spends much time heavily sleeping on a ship. Later he is carried around by a great fish and now he persists in being sedentary, seated in the bliss of shade. Hardly the life of an active prophet!

Jews were meant to be a light to the Gentiles. They were to attract nations to God. Yet Jonah had no light of care for Nineveh and the only attraction he thought reasonable between Nineveh and God was for Nineveh to attract and suffer God's condemnation.

One lesson that Jonah was about to be taught (among others) is a lesson I find hard to learn and harder to go on living it. The lesson is simply that we should care for neighbours. And who is our neighbour? The parable of the good Samaritan is one obvious definition and description of a neighbour (Luke 10:27–37). Another answer is contained in the words of a popular hymn provided by Tom Colvin and some young people from Ghana. Their words are matched to the tune of a local Ghanaian love song[9] —

> Jesu, Jesu: Fill us with your love,
> show us how to care
> for neighbours we have from you.

---

[9] Hymn No. 561 in *The Australian Hymn Book*, (Wm Collins Publishers Pty Ltd, Sydney).

Neighbours are black men and white
Neighbours are rich men and poor
Neighbours are nearby and far away

Neighbours are nearby and far away; for Jonah, as far as Nineveh. To care ungrudgingly for a people such as the Ninevites would have been extremely difficult; yet God's Spirit in us is a Spirit of care and loving kindness, and He is active to promote in us such care and kindness. The apostle Peter is someone who learned slowly of the need to love and care for Gentiles. In various ways the Spirit of God tutored Peter about this and, in later life, Peter was able to write to Jewish and Gentile Christians that "they should love one another deeply, from the heart." (1 Peter 1:22b). Peter writing to Gentiles and encouraging their love is a long way from Peter refusing to sit with them.

If I had to say which lesson I find most difficult and need to go on learning and remembering from the book of Jonah, it would be the lesson of caring for neighbours, especially those who are far away. In my culture, where being busy with the visible present is a daily recipe for many, it is ever so easy to let the mould of this culture squeeze out the care for those who are far away; even in spite of the greater electronic ease of communication.

Exclusive features of the culture of Israel and the appalling violence of Nineveh, perhaps together squeezed Jonah's heart such that it had no room for kindliness towards a menacing Nineveh. In the midst of Nineveh, Jonah's fondness was for those back in Israel not for the folk in Nineveh. His distaste for Nineveh coloured his perceptions. A symptom of his state of mind was his failure to be moved by the contrition of the Ninevites. He was so blinkered by his assessment of Nineveh that, in his eyes, it still deserved a crushing. Jonah's response to the people of Nineveh was coloured by their past not their present. He was chiefly responding to who they had been; not who they were now.

Jonah illustrated the behaviour of locking people in retrospect. Because the Ninevites had been cruel, they deserved punishment. But, as shown by God's benevolence, the current repentance of the Ninevites brought compassion from God. By contrast, their repentance and God's compassion drew an angry response from Jonah. Jonah was unable to appreciate their repentance because he mostly viewed them through their past. Care for people does not involve locking them in retrospect; viewing them *only* through their past. Noting change in people and properly discerning that change is part of caring for them.

There is a caution, however. Noting change does not infer that we should be prepared for and eager to accept all change in people, for not all change is worthy of support and embrace. Moreover, responding to people solely according to their seemingly changed behaviour has its own risks such as proneness to gullibility or being overly malleable; which is why I said the words 'properly discerning that change'. Identifying and understanding a person's *true* current nature and circumstance facilitates our care for them.

In verse 5 is described Jonah's response to the Ninevites. He chose not to draw near to them or celebrate their repentance. Rather he distanced himself from them and sat alone in anger. So as Jonah sat, waiting and fuming, God worked or, more importantly, the "LORD God" worked. In verse 6 of this last chapter, for the first time in the entire book, God is introduced as the "LORD God". This name for God is quite rare in the Old Testament. Only in the opening chapters of the book of Genesis is there other use of this title. The first use of the title is in Genesis 2:4 where we read of the "LORD God" creating the heavens and earth. The title continues to be used until the end of chapter 3 in Genesis where we read of God sending Adam and Eve from Eden's garden. What is the significance of the title?

Leupold (1942) says the title Yahweh Elohim (LORD God) suggests that the work God is about to do will display His mercy and His awe-inspiring power. Similarly, Griffith Thomas says the word Elohim specially refers to God's power and might. The word Yahweh or Jehovah, on the other hand, refers to God's activities of revelation and redemption. Putting the words together as the phrase "LORD God" yields the composite ideas of power and might, revelation and redemption. If we thus amplify verse 6 its beginning would read as:

> *Revelation and Redemption, Power and Might* prepared a vine and made it grow up over Jonah to give shade for his head.

The order of words is important. The intention and outcome is revelation and redemption: the visible means is power and might. That is, it is not a display of power and might for its own sake but rather for the purpose of revelation and redemption. This title for God indicates the purpose and nature of God's subsequent act is revelation and redemption. He will reveal to Jonah a rationale for His act of merciful kindness that Jonah will understand and appreciate. He will redeem Jonah initially from physical discomfort, but more important, redeem him from narrow-minded, self-centred thinking and carelessness. And the means to this revelation and redemption will be power and might. Jonah will experience God's power and authority over Nature: the plant, the worm and the wind are all His agents to teach Jonah. In God's hands they are the chalk and blackboard of Jonah's nature classroom.

In verse 6 we also read for the first time since his prayer of thanksgiving back in chapter two that Jonah is actually glad. For a time his prevalent feelings of displeasure and anger have subsided. In the book of Jonah, Jonah is seldom content or happy. Finally, here he is, glad for the shade. Further, if he sensed that God provided the shade, his gladness would arise, in part, from the knowledge that God wanted him to be comfortable while he waited and that therefore God was about to do something with Nineveh — perhaps destroy it!

Alas for Jonah; God was doing something with Jonah not Nineveh. Having previously appointed a large animal (a great fish) to rescue Jonah from death, God now turns to other end of the animal kingdom's size spectrum and selects a small worm to again rescue Jonah; this time from a corrosive hard-heartedness. God appoints this worm and the worm proceeds to behave naturally by feeding on Jonah's shade, killing the plant in the process. Persistently, earlier at sea and now on land, God uses Nature to challenge and teach Jonah about his nature. Next God sends a strong hot east wind. There were no clouds with this wind. The sun scorched down upon Jonah. As Jonah's discomfort rose, so did his anger and he told God about the extent of his anger when God asked him if his anger arose from the death of the plant (verse 9).

The Amplified Version outlines the narrative as follows. In verse 7 the Amplified Version states that at dawn "God provided (sent, prepared, appointed) a worm which chewed (ate, attacked, smote) the vine that it withered (died, dried up)." Then as described in verse 8, "God provided (sent, appointed, prepared, ordered) a scorching (hot, vehement, sultry) east wind, and the sun blazed on Jonah's head so that he grew faint." In response Jonah voiced that "It is better for me to die than to live." Then God asked Jonah "Do you have a right to be angry about the vine?" to which Jonah replied, "I do. I am angry enough to die."

Jonah was angry that this plant had died. It was a young, tender, productive and useful plant. The Hebrew phrase to describe the plant literally means "which was the son of a night and perished a son of the night." It is a Hebrew figurative phrase for perished rapidly. Jonah pitied this young plant eaten and killed in its prime. Jonah had more heart for a young plant than he had for a Ninevite child still to learn right from wrong, left from right. In effect God was saying; if you care for a plant yet to mature fully, should you not also at least care for Ninevite children yet to mature.

As an aside, when I first read and reacted to the book of Jonah, I wondered: How could God send a worm to destroy that which was living and was young and useful? I discovered that my question arose mostly from a me-centred view of Nature. All that the worm was doing was acting out laws and relationships already defined back in Genesis. It was not unnatural or wicked for the worm to live off the plant, be the plant young or old. Plants do not exist only for our benefit but for the rest of Nature as well. Our concern with Nature should not be limited by what only we can extract from it. All of God's creation, not just people, should share in the richness of creation. That is not to say that in God's presence plants and animals have the same status as people. Rather we should not cling to an exploitive and destructive attitude to Nature. Nature, not just mankind, should share in the bounty of creation. We are encouraged by Paul to be gentle (Ephesians 4:2), so should not our footsteps on this earth also be gentle?

Jonah pitied a plant that he apparently did not feed, protect or cause to grow. He enjoyed the benefit of the plant's shade but he had no investment in the care of the plant. By contrast, through the Nature He created and sustained, God cared for Nineveh and in Christ had an inestimable investment in their well-being. Surely, He had a right to pity Nineveh, its children and blameless cattle.

As a reflection I note that God's care is wide. It welcomes Ninevites, Jews and us. Remember the words of Christ: "Therefore go and make disciples of **all** nations." (Matthew 28:19a).

His care is never begrudging. It is His love and mercy at work. Remember the prayer of Daniel: "The Lord our God is merciful and forgiving, even though we have rebelled against Him." (Daniel 9:9). Even in the face of our sinfulness, God's love and mercy is at work.

By contrast, Jonah's care was blinkered; able to focus on the plant but not a repentant Ninevite. The fact that God laboured long to enable Jonah to see the Ninevites differently is a testament both to God's long-suffering and to how deep-seated some attitudes are. No doubt some of our attitudes need to be massaged or sometimes exploded to the surface before we see their error. Understanding that, I realise pain awaits me. It awaits us all. Yet arising from that pain can be the blessings of experience and hope, because of God's revealed and persistent love for us (Romans 5: 3–5).

What in the end God wished for Jonah was that he shared God's mercy for the Ninevites. Jonah would have known the Psalm "All the paths of the Lord are merciful" (Psalm 25:10). His difficulty was acknowledging that on one of God's paths of mercy lay Nineveh. Patiently God gives Jonah an understanding of His mercy.

The way God sought to teach Jonah has an echo in the interaction between Nathan (the prophet) and David (2 Samuel 12). Just as the worm was sent by God as an ingredient in Jonah's tuition, so God sent Nathan to David. Nathan told David a story that, similar to Jonah's reaction, led to David burning with anger (2 Samuel 12:1–4). Nathan and his story was the means God used to expose David's lack of compassion but more importantly the waywardness of his response to God. Similarly, God used a nature play and the actions of a worm to expose Jonah's lack of compassion for the Ninevites, but more importantly to expose the wayward nature of his response to God. Jonah was not thankful for God or worshipful of Him. He remained locked in anger towards God.

God wishes to be known and has committed much, including His only Son, so that we may more clearly comprehend Him. He asked questions of Jonah to help Jonah to think rather than be mired in emotion. God wished Jonah to comprehend His mercy. But why? To what end or effect?

Preachers and teachers with keen, tutored insight will offer more than the explanations I give, but I see at least two answers. Firstly, so that Jonah can be enabled to also be merciful. As said later in the New Testament, "Be ye therefore merciful, as your Father also is merciful" (Luke 6:36, KJV) or as Weymouth's translation says, "Be compassionate, just as your Father is compassionate."

Jonah's compassion for the plant was a seed for his understanding of God's compassion for Nineveh and, in turn, that was the beginning, however small, of any nascent compassion Jonah would have for the Ninevites.

God's care for Nineveh extended to its children *and* cattle. His compassion extended to those animals suffering from lack of food and water (Jonah 3:7). His mercy would allow those animals to once again be fed and watered.

A second explanation of why God wished Jonah to comprehend His mercy was simply that in the beginning and even at the end of all matters, it is His will and not Jonah's clouded and misshapen will that matters. In this case it is God's will to express His mercy towards the Ninevites. Yet Jonah's reaction to God was often based on *his* will; what *he* thought; what *he* perceived as fair and reasonable; what *he* wanted. Jonah, because of his will, was greatly annoyed that God's will, which differed from his own, would be expressed.

When one of the disciples asked Christ to teach them how to pray, one of the sets of words He gave them was "Your will be done on earth as it is in heaven." (Matthew 6:10). The disciples are taught to remember the centrality of God's will. In earnest prayer at the Mount of Olives Christ says "yet not my will, but yours be done." (Luke 22:42). God's will, His mercy, is expressed and God seeks to shift Jonah in his thinking, so that he can better understand God's actions and the centrality of God's will. With many words, patiently and persistently, God outlines to Jonah His will to be compassionate; a compassion so manifold that it extended even to Nineveh's cattle (Jonah 4:11).

FINAL COMMENTS

This last section is for reflections or comments not already made. The first is an observation that God responded to an entire city. His care was for a large city. If we are to be compassionate as the Lord is compassionate, then it is not unreasonable for us to care for groups of people, even groups as large as cities or regions or countries. To pray for a city or to be engaged in city-wide activity need not be an empty or fruitless task.

Secondly, Jonah illustrates how difficult it can be to be compassionate or forgiving. Storing up and dwelling on the bad behaviour and sins of people means those very things that we believe to be wrong end up filling our hearts. Yet remember the wisdom of Paul when he wrote: "whatever is true, whatever is noble, whatever is right, whatever is pure, whatever is lovely, whatever is admirable—if anything is excellent or praiseworthy—think about such things." (Philippians 4:8). By not carrying in us a spirit of forgiveness we expose ourselves to being filled with the very negativity and darkness that we so strongly condemn in others. Remember the words in the Lord's prayer: "forgive us our shortcomings, as we also have forgiven those who have failed in their duty towards us." (Matthew 6:12, Weymouth). The Spirit of God knits in us a spirit of forgiveness which we must exercise and keep on deciding to exercise. For those yet to be deeply or horribly harmed by others, forgiveness may seem a simple task. Those crushed or battered by darkness have a more difficult, yet in the end, perhaps richer journey to forgiveness.

Thirdly, the book of Jonah reveals reciprocity in God's relationships with us (see James 4:8). The people of Nineveh draw near to God and He draws near to them with compassion. God draws near to Jonah and wishes

Jonah to once again draw near to Him. Elsewhere in the Old Testament king David seeks to build God's house and so God promises to build up his house. Such reciprocity is often a feature of God's dealings with people. The personal implication is clear; genuinely drawing near to God does not yield rejection, rather compassion. As said in Isaiah 42:3, "A bruised reed He will not break, and a smouldering wick he will not snuff out." We are that weakened, tarnished reed. We are that dim, smoky effulgence.

Fourthly, the wickedness of Nineveh brought response from God. It is the same for each of us. We may not be cruel like the Ninevites; but each of us, against the measure of God's law, stands with the Ninevites as law-breakers. Just like the Ninevites, our skills, our wealth, our character may be impressive to other people — that's a sociological reality, but in the end none of that washes with God. Before God each of us is a law-breaker: all are flawed in some way; "all have sinned" (Romans 3:23). Yet through the love of Jesus Christ, God has responded to *our* wickedness. Like the wickedness of Nineveh, our wickedness matters to God.

Our carelessness, our selfishness, our heartlessness, our sloth or our relentless business and preoccupation with the less important — they all matter to God. This is not to say that because our frailties and wickedness matter to God that we should sin more, so that we will somehow matter more to God. Those ideas are the sorts of lies Paul refuted. No; our frailties matter to God so that people should bring them to the One to whom it deeply matters. "Come to me, all you who are weary and burdened, and I will give you rest" says Christ (Matthew 11:28). We should take the burden of our shortcomings, harm and wickedness to God and not sit in Bunyan's slough of despair or a guilt-ridden mire of self-pity. And having brought what weakens and poisons us to Him, we should then move on to listen and be taught and led by the Good Shepherd, the One who loves and cares for us.

Fifthly, our lives are full of journeys and learnings. We are invited to come, to stay, to go, to travel alone or in company. Our journeys are uncertain. We know not how long the shade lasts before a worm or a hot wind appears. We know not the day when the storm will arrive, nor if we are to drown or to be saved. In the midst of these journeys there are learnings. Our teachers are many and varied, not just people, not just scripture.

Sixthly, from what is written about Jonah it seems that he was often alone. We read of no friend, no family member or servant accompanying him. Yet his solitude, his private prayer and complaining, now are shared with all who bother to read the scriptures. In that sense, like Jonah, we never know what becomes of our lone acts; what stays hidden or what is exposed.

Although alone it appears that Jonah was not crippled by loneliness. He seems at ease with being single and is prepared to be single-minded in wanting harm to Nineveh. There is no friend or colleague to challenge his thinking or question his motives. The voices of strangers, the sailors, are the source of his chastisement rather than the comments of caring family members or friends. In fleeing to Tarshish he was also avoiding any opportunity to hear the wise counsel of others who loved him; or perhaps back in Zebulun he had already dismissed such advice and care. Either the absence of advice from people close to Jonah or his dismissal of such sound advice is, however, no impediment to God instructing Jonah. God turns to Nature to be Jonah's teacher.

Seventhly, scripture at times is unflinchingly honest in its exposure of people. Often laid bare before us, as readers, is the frailty, the worst and best of humanity. Jonah has no privacy. Down through the centuries eyes have poured over his story, provided by the writer of Jonah and used by the Spirit of God for our instruction. Whilst needing to be respectful of their frank exposure, we should not hide or sugar-coat the behaviour and nature of those given to us in scripture.

Eighthly, and an expansion of the previous point, prophets such as Jonah are people. Jonah knew anguish, disappointment, separation, death, cruelty, gladness, discomfort and mercy. God's servants, special though they are, often with richness of insight, power and courage, nonetheless remain human. Even now God's servants, be they lay-folk or clerics, are all human.

Clerics especially are exposed occasionally to unreasonable expectations and demands from the laity they serve. The humanity and frailties of clerics are often hidden from public view, lest the public be offended or unduly disappointed. Clerics, like those whom they serve, also need care and understanding. The poem *The Minister* implies as much:

ROSS KINGWELL, PH.D.

The Minister

'The pleasure's in the giving,' he said
with tired eyes that told the lie.

He'd given too much to those
who'd given up,
were giving up,
were given up
to themselves. RK, 1997

Ninthly, it is unfortunately fairly commonplace for Old Testament characters like Jonah to remain as cartoon-like characters in our memories, for we rarely re-visit their stories through literate digging and reflection. Hence, we grow into adulthood without being able to draw upon any deeper and richer insights about the person of Jonah and God's response to him. So Jonah sits on a mental shelf, like so many bibles, rarely opened in spite of the riches within its pages.

Lastly, although the book of Jonah illustrates the power of God, reflected in the way He directs Nature be it sea, wind, great fish, plant or worm, it does not follow that always He will ensure we are protected from the forces of Nature. The forces of gravity, wind and wave continue to leave their mark on the earth, including on us who dwell on the earth. Hence, being subject to those forces, we can be advantaged or disadvantaged by them. Trusting that God will use His power over Nature to ensure we have a safe, long-lived existence is a false hope. What is a certain hope is that He will prepare a table for us in the presence of our enemies (Psalm 23:5). Those enemies are all that would harm us in our walk with God, including disease, ailment, tragedy, destructive attitudes and woeful behaviour. So in the face of natural and even self-induced calamity He will sustain and feed us, the good Shepherd that He is. Note this does not mean calamity will not occur nor should we seek out calamity; but rather in its midst He will steadfastly care for us; reproving, teaching, leading and maturing us, pouring His love into our hearts (Romans 5:3–5).

BIBLIOGRAPHY

Allen, Leslie C. 1976. "The Books of Joel, Obadiah, Jonah and Micah." In *The New International Commentary on the Old Testament*, edited by R.K. Harrison, Grand Rapids, Michigan: William B. Eerdmans Publishing Company.

Beck, Bruce N. 2000. Exegetical and Theological Trajectories from the book of Jonah in Jewish and Christian Sources, Doctor of Theology dissertation, Cambridge, Massachusetts: Harvard Divinity School, Harvard University.

Bedford, Peter. 2005. "The economy of the near east in the first millennium BC." In *The ancient economy: evidence and models*, edited by J.G. Manning and I. Morris, 58–83. Stanford: Stanford University Press.

Carlisle, Thomas J. 1968. *You Jonah*. Poems by T.J. Carlisle, Grand Rapids, Michigan: William B. Eerdmans Publishing Company.

Crean, Thomas. 2002. "On the prophet Jonah." *The Roman Theological Forum*, No. 101, September 2002.

Davis, Edward B. 1991. *A modern Jonah*. Available at: http://www.reasons.org/articles/a-modern-jonah

Delitzsch, Franz. 1973. *Commentary on Isaiah Volume 7*. Grand Rapids, Michigan: William B. Eerdmans Publishing Company.

Douglas, James D. 1962. *The New Bible Dictionary*, edited by J.D. Douglas, F.F. Bruce, J.I. Packer, R.V.G. Tasker and D.J. Wiseman. London: Inter-Varsity Press.

Ellul, Jacques. 1971. *The Judgement of Jonah*. Grand Rapids, Michigan: William B. Eerdmans Publishing Company.

Feinberg, Charles L. 1948. *The Minor Prophets*. Chicago: Moody Press.

Gaebelein, Frank E. 1970. *Four Minor Prophets: Their message for today*, William B. Eerdmans Publishing Company, Grand Rapids, Michigan: Moody Press.

Hailey, Homer. 1972. *A Commentary on the Minor Prophets*. Grand Rapids, Michigan: Baker Book House.

Henry, Leslie. 2012. *The Historicity of the Book of Jonah*. Xulon Press, USA.

Hercus, John. 1965. *More Pages from God's Case-book*. London: Inter-Varsity Fellowship Press.

Jacobsen, Thorkild, and Lloyd, S. 1935. "Sennacherib's Aqueduct at Jerwan." University of Chicago. *Oriental Institute Publications* 24.

Keil, Carl. F. 1973. *Commentary on the Minor Prophets* Volume 10. Grand Rapids, Michigan: William B. Eerdmans Publishing Company.

Kendall, Robert T. 1978. *Jonah: Sermons preached at Westminster Chapel*. London: Hodder and Stoughton.

Laetsch, Theodore. 1956. *The Minor Prophets*. Bible Commentary, Missouri: Concordia Publishing House.

Leupold, Herbert C. 1942. *Exposition of Genesis Volume 1*. London: The Wartburg Press and the Evangelical Press.

Lewis, Charles S. 1958. *Reflections on the Psalms*. London: Fontana Books.

Martin, Hugh. 1870. *Jonah*, 1966 reprint by The Geneva series of commentaries. London: The Banner of Truth Trust.

Massa, Aldo. 1977. *The World of the Phoenicians*. Geneva: Minerva S.A.

Niemöller, Martin. 1989. "Als die Nazis die Kommunisten holten," poem attributed to Martin Niemöller; translation in *Time* Magazine, August 28, 1989.

Postgate, J. Nicholas. 1979. "The economic structure of the Assyrian Empire." In *Power and propaganda: a symposium on ancient empires*, edited by M.T. Larsen. Copenhagen: Akademisk Forlag.

Radner, Karen. 2000. "How did the Neo-Assyrian king perceive his land and its resources?" In *Rainfall and agriculture in northern Mesopotamia: proceedings of the 3rd MOS symposium*, edited by R.M. Jas, Leiden, 233–246, May 21–22, 1999. Leiden: Nederlands Instituut voor het Nabije Oosten.

Smith, James E. 2011. *Obadiah, Joel, Jonah, Micah: A Christian Interpretation*. Florida: Florida Christian College.

Stronach, David. 1994. "Village to metropolis: Nineveh and the beginnings of urbanism in northern Mesopotamia." In *Nuove fondazioni nel Vicino Oriente Antico: Realtà e ideologia*, edited by S. Mazzoni, 85–114.Pisa: Giardini.

Wilkinson, Tony J., Wilkinson, E.B., Ur, J. and Altaweel, M. 2005. "Landscape and settlement in the neo-Assyrian empire." *Bulletin of the American Schools of Oriental Research* 340: 23–55.

NOTES

NOTES

NOTES

NOTES

NOTES

NOTES

NOTES

NOTES

NOTES

NOTES

NOTES

NOTES

NOTES

NOTES

NOTES

NOTES

NOTES

NOTES

NOTES

NOTES

NOTES

NOTES

Ross Kingwell is a professor of agricultural economics at the University of Western Australia. He is a distinguished fellow of the Australasian Agricultural and Resource Economics Society and chief economist at the Australian Export Grains Innovation Centre. However, as he readily admits, when it comes to theology or scripture, he heralds no formal qualification or academic prowess. Yet in spite of this amateur status, his study of scripture, as revealed in this book, is nonetheless thorough, serious and insightful.